SPOOKY
Great Smokies

Tales of Hauntings, Strange Happenings,
and Other Local Lore

RETOLD BY S. E. SCHLOSSER

ILLUSTRATED BY PAUL G. HOFFMAN

Globe
Pequot

GUILFORD, CONNECTICUT

Globe Pequot

An imprint of Globe Pequot, the trade division of
The Rowman & Littlefield Publishing Group, Inc.
4501 Forbes Blvd., Ste. 200
Lanham, MD 20706
GlobePequot.com

Distributed by NATIONAL BOOK NETWORK

Text copyright © 2021 S. E. Schlosser
Illustration's copyright © 2021 Paul G. Hoffman

All rights reserved. No part of this book may be reproduced in any form or by
any electronic or mechanical means, including information storage and retrieval
systems, without written permission from the publisher, except by a reviewer
who may quote passages in a review.

British Library Cataloguing in Publication Information Available

Library of Congress Cataloging-in-Publication Data Available

Names: Schlosser, S. E., author. | Hoffman, Paul G., illustrator.
Title: Spooky Great Smokies : tales of hauntings, strange happenings, and
    other local lore / retold by S. E. Schlosser ; illustrated by Paul G.
    Hoffman.
Description: Guilford, Connecticut : Globe Pequot, [2021] | Includes
    bibliographical references. | Summary: "From the farmer who finds a
    Cavern of Skulls to a moonshiner who makes a deal with a water demon,
    and the Half Shaved ghost seeking vengeance to the first (and only)
    meeting of the Asheville Ghost Club, the Great Smoky Mountains and its
    foothills abound with spooky tales"— Provided by publisher.
Identifiers: LCCN 2021014991 (print) | LCCN 2021014992 (ebook) | ISBN
    9781493044832 (paperback) | ISBN 9781493044849 (epub)
Subjects: LCSH: Ghosts—Great Smoky Mountains (N.C. and Tenn.) | Haunted
    places—Great Smoky Mountains (N.C. and Tenn.)
Classification: LCC BF1472.U6 S2955 2021 (print) | LCC BF1472.U6 (ebook)
    | DDC 133.1/2976889—dc23
LC record available at https://lccn.loc.gov/2021014991
LC ebook record available at https://lccn.loc.gov/2021014992

♾™ The paper used in this publication meets the minimum requirements of
American National Standard for Information Sciences—Permanence of Paper
for Printed Library Materials, ANSI/NISO Z39.48-1992

For my family: David, Dena, Tim, Arlene, Hannah, Seth, Emma, Nathan, Ben, Deb, Gabe, Clare, Jack, Chris, Karen, Davey, and Aunt Mil.

For Valerie, Efren, Brian and Brendan Pedrozo. Thanks for being such wonderful friends.

And for Paul Hoffman, Erin Turner, and all the wonderful folks at Globe Pequot Press, with my thanks.

Contents

PART TWO: POWERS OF DARKNESS AND LIGHT

Introduction

The view was stunning. Layer upon layer of misty blue mountains stretched out before me in a vast panorama. Standing at the top of the Clingmans Dome Observation Tower, I could see over 100 miles in every direction. A cold wind whipped my hair into my eyes and made my teeth chatter. I hurried to zip my coat and pull up my hood before snapping several photos of the Frasier firs that dominated the peak.

For a moment, I had the observation tower to myself. Several folks were hiking up the steep paved path from the parking lot, but none had reached the massive curving ramp that led to the top of the tower. I took a deep breath of the cold air and leaned against the railing, basking in the beauty before me.

Somewhere on this mountain, the Cherokee martyr Tsali and his family had sheltered in a cave after escaping from the soldiers who forcibly removed them from their home. Tsali sacrificed his life to ensure that his people would always have a place to call home in these Great Smoky Mountains, and his spirit is said to linger in this place, watching over his people ("The Watcher").

After descending the spiraling ramp, I headed to my car and drove down the mountain toward Mingus Mill and the Mountain Farm Museum. As I entered the Oconaluftee River Valley, I mused on the many spooky stories attached to this region. My favorite is a "Jack Tale" in which Jack takes a job at a cursed mill and twelve creepy black cats pay him a visit ("The Cat's Paw").

Then there are the Cherokee tales that describe the Uktena, a massive snake that haunts the remote mountain passes and mountain peaks ("The Scale") and the fearsome Spear-Finger, who roamed all over the Smoky Mountains murdering villagers with her sharp stone digit.

After a stop at the visitor center, I took a stroll through the Mountain Farm Museum. A quilt in the old farmhouse reminded me of a fatal wedding gift given to a boyfriend-stealing bride ("The Curse"). And a wooden seat in the front room looked eerily similar to a certain vampire chair that is said to be making the rounds of antiques shops and flea markets in Gatlinburg and other East Tennessee towns ("The Mule-Eared Chair").

Indeed, the eastern side of the Smokies abounds with spooky tales, like the story of a shadow woman who appeared to a farmer each morning and evening to beg for a cup of milk. Skinned Tom is another East Tennessee haunt, though his is a sinister tale that warns the unfaithful to steer clear of local lover's lanes for their illicit trysting.

From the farmer who finds a cavern of skulls, to a moonshiner who makes a deal with a water demon, and the half-shaved ghost seeking vengeance to the first (and only) meeting of the Asheville Ghost Club, the Great Smoky Mountains and its foothills abound with spooky tales. My favorites are in this collection.

—Sandy Schlosser

PART ONE
Ghost Stories

1

Shadow Woman

SEVIER COUNTY, TENNESSEE

"It's terrible sad, a nice girl like Tilly dyin' so young," my wife said as she kneaded dough on our big kitchen table. "The neighbor said they buried her in the cemetery this mornin' with her new baby in her arms. I remember Tilly when she was just a little girl, splashin' in the creek with her sisters and a making a right mess of her Sunday-go-to-meeting dress."

"It sure is sad," I replied distractedly. We'd just returned from a week's visit with our boy down in Knoxville, and my mind was preoccupied by a bad cough Old Sal had developed while we were away. I wondered if I should ask Granny should have a look, since she was a right hand at animal doctoring.

I was pulled from my thoughts when a soft clod of dough bounced off my nose. I rubbed the spot sheepishly and looked across the table at my grinning wife of nigh on twenty-five years.

"You weren't listenin' to me," she said, an oft-heard complaint. "You're thinkin' about your nanny goat again!"

I chuckled. "Are you jealous of a goat?" I asked, fulfilling my part of the daily ritual.

"If'n I ever leave you, it's on account of that there goat," my bride said with a wink. "You think more 'bout her than you do 'bout me."

"She's got a cough," I said defensively.

"Probably somethin' she ate," said my wife. "She'll throw it up eventually, like she always does. Now get out to that barn and get the milkin' done. It's near dinnertime!"

I brought in the cows and settled into the evening chores. I was just setting myself down to milk the cows when a shadow blocked the barn doorway. I looked up and saw a slim woman silhouetted against the evening sun. She was wearing a raggedy black dress and I couldn't make out her face in the dim light of the barn.

"Hello?" I called uncertainly. I thought I knew everyone hereabouts, but I didn't recognize this silent figure. The woman held a tin cup in her thin hand. She stretched it out toward me in such a pleading manner that I took it at once and filled it with fresh milk.

"There you go," I said, returning it to her hand.

She turned and walked out of the barn, vanishing into the final sunbeams of the day without saying a word.

"It was strange," I told my wife over dinner. "I don't know where she came from or where she went. She was just there and then gone again."

"It's probably one of the folks from over the hill whose cow's gone dry," she said calmly.

"Maybe," I said doubtfully. I was pretty good at keeping track of folks hereabouts. This shadow woman wasn't someone I knew. Or was she? I tried to chase down a vague memory, but it escaped me.

"How's your goat?" asked my wife. All thoughts of the shadow woman vanished as I described in minute detail the hacking cough old Sal had made—twice—when I brought her into the barn.

I was up at sunrise to milk the cows, and the shadow woman was back too. She didn't respond to any of my questions, she just held out her cup and waited for me to fill it. Even in daylight, a shadow veiled her face; a fact that made the hairs on my neck prickle. I worried over the matter most of the day as I went about my chores. Between old Sal's cough and the shadow woman, it was a miracle I got any work done.

"Stop your frettin'," my wife advised as she pegged out the washing on the line. "I heard that cough of old Sal's and it's the same one she always gets when she eats somethin' she shouldn't. There's guilt in that cough, mark my words. The last time I heard it, she ate your favorite blue shirt."

Old Sal was still hacking away when I brought the stock into the barn that evening. *I'll have to ask Granny to come over and doctor her*, I thought as I reached for the milk stool. All at once, the shadow lady stood beside me with her cup. There was an air of urgency about her this evening that gave me the jitters. I watched her vanish into the setting sun with her cup of milk and frowned with concern. Something was wrong.

"Why does she need a cup of milk every morning and evening?" I asked my wife after dinner.

My wife thought on this question for a piece, then said: "I don't know. But I think we should find out. You should follow her to see where she's going with the cup. If'n we find out who she is, we can figure out how to help without injurin' her pride."

SHADOW WOMAN

The shadow woman appeared with her cup as soon as I entered the barn the next morning. I filled it with warm milk and watched her disappear out the barn door. Then I tiptoed after her, using my best coon-tracking skills to keep her from suspecting she was being followed.

The shadow woman walked up the road a-piece, and the further we went the more nervous I got. There wasn't anything there but the cemetery. Why would she go there?

The slim figure glided past the laurel thicket and into the graveyard. I followed whisper-silent behind. The shadow woman walked toward a headstone marking a freshly dug grave and vanished inside with her cup.

I just about had me a heart attack. "Lord Almighty," I gasped, reeling backward. I'd been giving milk to a ha'nt! But why did a ghost need a cup of milk? It didn't make sense. Then I remembered my wife telling me about a Cove girl and her newborn baby who'd been buried on the day we got back from Knoxville. That was also the first night the shadow woman came to our barn to ask me for a cup of milk.

A bolt of pure fear set my feet a running. I lit down that road faster than a man with a bear chasing him.

"Mildred!" I shouted as I skidded into the yard. "Mildred!"

My wife stomped across the yard, waving something frilly and torn. "My best drawers," she roared. "That old goat of yours ate my best drawers! She just threw them up again and they're ruined." She stopped abruptly when she saw my pale face. "What's ailing you?" she demanded, dropping her ruined knickers into the waiting jaws of old Sal, who'd followed her from the barn.

"That shadow woman! It's Tilly. Her ha'nt came back from the grave to feed the baby. It's still alive!"

Mildred gaped at me for a moment. Then she snapped: "What you waitin' for? Get a shovel and your carpentry tools and we'll call on the neighbors. You can't dig that grave up by your lone self."

We recruited the neighbors and went to the cemetery to dig up the grave. It was hard work, but fear motivated us. Before long, we could hear the whimpers of the poor little baby buried alive with its dead mama. Thank the Almighty, we were in time to save it.

It took some doing, prying the lid off that coffin. But at last, we were looking down into the sweet dead face of Tilly, the shadow lady. A small whimpering bundle was nestled in her arms and a tin cup full of warm milk lay beside her.

2

That Old Church

SERVIERVILLE, TENNESSEE

When Granny marched into the mayor's office, folks in town knew he was in a heap of trouble. Nobody messed with Granny when she had a bee in her bonnet, and boy howdy was there a gleam in her eye that morning. As word spread, folks took to eavesdropping under the open window as Granny lit into the mayor about the old church building that was shaming the town. It was so run-down that the congregation took to meeting in homes instead.

"But Granny, everyone knows its ha'nted," the mayor protested.

"I don't care if the devil hisself is livin' in the belfry," Granny said. "It t'aint right and your goin' to fix it."

The poor mayor was beet red by the time Granny got done scolding him, and a new sign was pasted up around the town, advertising a $500 reward for anyone who would spend the night in the old church to prove it wasn't haunted.

'Course, everyone knew it weren't true. If you visited that old church at twilight, a body could see strange lights flickering and glimpse pale figures floating inside the sanctuary. Ha'nts walked right through the wood of the creaky old pews jest as if they weren't setting there. And when the moonlight shone through the church windows, things really got lively in that old church. It gave folks the jitters and nobody in town wanted $500 worth of trouble.

But then a young feller rode into town on a fancy horse, and he seemed right interested in the mayor's sign. "I'm not scared of ghosts," the young feller told the mayor. "I'll spend the night in that old church and prove it isn't haunted."

"Suit yourself," the mayor said.

The young feller got himself some victuals for his dinner and carried them to that old church to eat. It was so full of dust and cobwebs that it set the young feller to sneezing. He wiped his streaming nose and used his handkerchief to dust off one of them worn-out pews. Then he set himself down to his meal.

It was full-dark by the time he finished his meal, so he lit a lantern, put on his nightshirt and night cap, and made a bed on the pew. He pulled out a book to read and made himself comfortable, propping his feet on the armrest in a most irreverent manner. It must have made the ha'nts mad, cause a moment later something knocked him right off the pew. The young feller screeched as he landed in the small space between the pew where he was setting and the one right in front of it.

"What the hel . . . I mean heck!" The young feller realized he was in church and changed his cuss word in the nick of time. But the ha'nts weren't having none of it. He found himself staring up at the floating blue head of an angry ghost-woman. Her eyes were flashing sparks at him for cussing. He yelped like a young 'un and scrambled under the pew to get away.

When he peered out of his hiding place, the young feller found himself nose-to-nose with a cloudy ghost whose neck was

THAT OLD CHURCH

severed. Blood poured gruesomely from the open wound. The young feller wailed and sprang up on the seat of the pew, ready to run for his life. But two ha'nts in their worn-out Sunday best surrounded the young feller and a big black dog with red eyes blocked the front door, his glowing eyes fixed on the intruder. An eerie wail of organ music proceeded the appearance of a withered corpse in a bride's gown, who marched down the aisle holding a blackened bouquet. Everywhere the young feller looked, there were ha'nts. There was even a preacher-man floating near the pulpit.

The young feller knew he had to escape from them ha'nts before he lost his mind. He made a mighty leap off the pew and landed in the aisle, ready to run. As soon as his foot touched the floor, all the ha'nts straightened up and stared out the broken windows of the church. The young feller looked that way too, his skin crawling. In the moonlight, he could see the old tombstones in the church cemetery.

Something stirred among the graves, and the young feller's blood went cold. He tried to run, but his feet were frozen to the warped old floorboards. The black dog whined deep in its throat, and the young feller knew that whatever was skeering them ha'nts must be truly awful.

A glowing skeleton appear above a gravestone and marched gravely toward the church. It was followed by another skeleton, and then another one. Soon, a long line of skeletons glided through the church wall and marched over the old wooden pews as if they weren't setting there. When the lead skeleton reached the center aisle, he turned sharply and walked toward the intruder. Fear finally unlocked the young feller's knocking knees.

He screamed and whirled hisself toward the front door. But a line of skeletons was marching up behind him. He was trapped!

There must be something he could do. But what? The young feller glanced around desperate-like, and spied the sturdy wooden offering plates at the end of each pew. Maybe he could throw those at the skeletons? It might distract them long enough for him to run away.

Then a clever thought struck him. He was an educated man, and in this desperate moment he put that book-learning to good use. The young feller thrust the offering plates toward the marching skeletons and said: "Amen, brothers and sisters! It's time to take up the collection." Waving at the other ghosts, he shouted: "Everyone, take out your wallets. We must tithe before the Almighty."

The thought of parting with their money did not set well with them ghosts. The skeletons vanished instantly with a great popping sound and a ghostly wind that blew the young feller's night cap clean off. The ha'nted congregants wailed in dismay and faded away, until only the preacher was left. The preacher looked sadly around the decrepit church and shook his head at such miserly behavior. He faded sadly away.

So, the young feller got rid of the ha'nts in that old church and won the $500, fair and square. And everyone in the valley turned out to fix up that old church, good as new. From that day on, folks in that congregation were plenty generous in their giving, 'cause none of them fancied the notion of coming back as a stingy skeleton in the hereafter.

3

The Gift

We sat looking at the casket as the preacher spoke a few words to comfort the bereaved. My cousin Ethel wept softly, clinging to her young 'uns who were still stunned by the loss of their father. A fever took Jimmy way too early, and the whole community mourned with the family.

My wife, Martha, gave Ethel a hug and kiss once the burial was over, and I patted her shoulder awkwardly.

"You'll stay for supper?" Ethel asked us. "Jimmy had something he wanted me to give to you."

A gift? That surprised me, but I should have expected it. Jimmy and I were close as kin. We grew up together in the Cataloochee Valley and Jimmy first met Ethel at my house when she came to visit my folks. I'd been best man at their wedding.

"A neighbor's daughter is watching our boys, so we can stay as long as you want," Martha said.

Ethel's small house was overflowing with family and neighbors. My wife went straight to the kitchen to help set out the food while a couple of us did chores to help the new widow.

13

After dinner, Ethel led me outside to Jimmy's "office." It was just a fixed-up corner in the old woodshed, but Jimmy and I'd spent many a happy hour there drinking and relaxing whenever the house got too loud. I had to blink hard to keep from crying when Ethel walked me back there.

Ethel went to the fancy carved desk Jimmy had made with his own hands and pulled a pistol out of the drawer. That did me in completely. I sat down and wept worse than the young 'uns. Jimmy was right proud of that pistol. He'd bought it about a month ago from a tourist who came to the valley to fish and never got to use it. Jimmy took sick that same evening and the gun had set out in the woodshed office ever since.

"Your boy should have that pistol," I told Ethel, wiping my eyes.

"No," she said at once. "Jimmy wanted you to have something of his. When the boy asked for his Pa's rifle, Jimmy said to give you this to remember him by."

What could I say? It was too much, but I could tell from my cousin's face that protesting would offend her. I accepted the pistol.

Ethel nodded as if she could read my thoughts. "There's plenty of bears and wild panthers out there. Carrying a pistol is a good idea when you are walking outside after dark," she said.

"Yes ma'am. It will come in handy this evening when I escort my missus home," I said, rising from the chair. "Something I need to do right now, as it happens. It's near dark and we've got a few miles to cover."

Martha and I said goodbye to Ethel and walked out to the road. I showed my wife the pistol Jimmy gave me as we walked toward our home on the far side of the valley. Then I put it into my pocket and took her hand like we were still courting. It wasn't often I got to step out with my bride without our young 'uns in tow. We'd been wed for many years, but I still knew how to make her giggle and blush.

We were about a mile from our place when a strange man appeared, walking silently next to my wife in the twilight. That was odd. Neither of us heard him approach. He was just suddenly there. I called a greeting, but he didn't answer. I gripped the pistol in my pocket, not sure if the fellow was shy or if he was a troublemaker. Folks often joined up with a group for safety's sake, especially if they were walking alone after dark. But generally, a fellow would introduce himself and talk to the people he was accompanying. This silent stranger raised goose bumps on my arms and legs. Something wasn't quite right. On the other hand, he wasn't threatening us, and having a third person with us helped keep the bears and panthers at bay. I'd just keep my eye on him.

I was so busy minding my thoughts that I stumbled over a rock in the road. The stranger stumbled at the same moment. That was bizarre. Martha and I exchanged confused glances. Was the stranger deliberately mimicking me, or was it just a coincidence? I shrugged, and so did the stranger. I stopped. So did the stranger. When I continued, the stranger did too. Martha stared back and forth between us, perplexed by the strangeness of the man's behavior.

To confirm my suspicions, I pointed toward the bend in the road and said: "We're nearly at our turnoff." The stranger pointed at the same moment and his mouth moved, but no words came out.

"Why is he acting so strange?" Martha whispered, but I didn't have an answer.

"Just keep going," I murmured. "If he follows us into the yard, I'll make him leave."

We quickened our pace and turned off at the bend in the road. The stranger followed us. Martha's lips tightened and I patted the pocket containing the pistol to reassure her. Then I hurried my wife into the house and turned to confront the stranger, pistol in hand. He was gone. I searched the yard and all the outbuildings, but the stranger had vanished.

The presence of a stranger in the vicinity made me nervous, so I walked the neighbor's daughter home and warned her folks about the stranger before I went to check on the livestock. Then I locked up the house good and tight and put the pistol next to the bed before we went to sleep.

It was almost midnight when a breeze blew the covers off me and Martha, startling us awake.

"What in tarnation?" I shouted, clutching for the bedclothes, which were tangled at the foot of the bed.

The stranger walked into our bedroom and marched to the foot of the bed. Martha screamed and I jumped out of bed, waving my pistol. Instantly, the stranger vanished.

"The boys," Martha cried. She ran to check on the young 'uns. I was right on her heels. The boys were sleeping peacefully in the loft. The stranger was nowhere to be seen.

I lit the lamp and we checked the door. The bolts were still engaged and there was no sign of a forced entry.

"Did he come through a window?" she asked.

"See for yourself," I said, gesturing to the wooden shutters I'd pulled tight before bed. Martha tested each one, but they

THE GIFT

were still locked. Her face was pale when she looked me in the eye.

"Is it a ha'nt?" she asked.

"I think so," I replied. "I don't know what else it could be."

We went back to bed, both of us shaking with nerves. I didn't think I would fall asleep, but I must have, because I was startled awake when the bedroom door opened a second time and a breeze shook the room. As before, the stranger walked right up to our bed.

I knew my ha'nt stories. You were supposed to talk to the ghost to find out why it was ha'nting you. I sat bolt upright and grabbed the pistol. Pointing it at the spirit, I said: "Who are you and what do you want?"

The stranger didn't reply. He just faded away, as before.

Martha was watching this second encounter with wide eyes. She said: "I think the ha'nt is tied to that gun. It showed up right after we left Ethel's place and now it's coming into the bedroom to look for the pistol."

"Why would Ethel give us a ha'nted gun?" I asked, lighting the lamp so we could study the pistol. There were no scratch marks or initials or something that would give us a clue to its previous ownership.

"She probably didn't know about the ghost. Didn't you say that Jimmy never used it?" Martha replied.

"That's right," I said. "He got sick before he could try it out. And he kept it in his woodshed office, so the spirit would have stayed back there. No wonder Jimmy got such a good price for the pistol. That tourist was trying to get rid of the ha'nt."

"You'd best put that pistol in *our* woodshed for the night or we won't get any sleep," said Martha firmly. "And you are selling the gun in the morning. No arguments."

The ghost fell into step beside me as soon as I exited the house and it accompanied me to the woodshed.

"Sorry, stranger. No fancy office here," I said, putting the gun in a notch under the roof. "We will find you a new home in the morning."

The ghost didn't say a word. It just strode into the woodshed and the door slammed shut in a supernatural gust of wind.

I was going to Tennessee in the morning to take care of some family business. I'd sell the pistol when I got there. I hoped Jimmy wouldn't mind me selling his memorial gift. If he did, his ha'nt just might pay us a visit. Still, better Jimmy than an unknown ghost, I decided, leaving the spirit and its gun in the woodshed and heading back to bed.

4

The Phantom of Middlebrook Pike

KNOXVILLE, TENNESSEE

I fingered the letter in my pocket as I strolled along Middlebrook Pike on a sunny afternoon in the fall of 1894. The letter was from an old war buddy of mine who fought and bled next to me on the battlefield. Our bond remained strong in the years that followed and we corresponded often. This letter had been sent to me from my old friend's deathbed. I thought I knew all his secrets, but its contents surprised me. I'd memorized the text and reviewed it in my mind as I strolled under the trees amidst the dappled afternoon sunlight.

Dear Danny,

By the time you read this, I will be gone. After surviving the war, who would guess that I'd fall at last to pneumonia? You were always my best pal, and I want you to have a little something of mine, if you can find it.

There was still plenty of fighting and raiding going on when I got home. Not everyone believed the war was over. One afternoon, I heard shouts and smelled smoke. A group of marauders were plundering the neighborhood. I had hidden all my war earnings and a pile of gold my late father left me underneath a loose floorboard. There was no way the raiders would miss it when they came through. I swept the money into a bag and went running through the woods, trying to stay ahead of the marauders. I heard them invade my house, so I picked up speed. But they spotted me through the window and followed me into the woods.

The sack of gold was weighing me down, so I slung the sack into a handy hole at the roots of a large tree and thrust my red-handled pocketknife underneath a large branch to mark the place so I could find it again. Then I hightailed it out of there and made my way to safety, but not before those goldurned raiders put a bullet in my hip. I've been crippled ever since, so I couldn't retrieve my father's gold. It's too late for me now, so I am passing it along to you, my best pal. I don't want the money falling to anyone else, so I'll send my spirit back to watch over the treasure until you come.

I was a bit of a fool and mentioned the gold to several folks who've been tending me while I was ill. Of course, rumors are everywhere now. They'll probably dig up the whole forest when I'm gone, trying to find the money. But I didn't tell them about my marker. You're the only one that knows about it.

Good luck.

Benjamin

I was traveling when the letter arrived, and my wife set it aside for me. In the flurry of homecoming, she forgot all about the letter and it lay in an old drawer for several years before a thorough housecleaning revealed it. By the time the letter reached my hand, so many years had passed that I was certain treasure hunters had long since dug up my friend's gold. But to honor his memory, I planned a trip to Knoxville.

On my first night in town, I took a seat at the bar in a local tavern and gathered rumors about Middlebrook Pike. There were plenty of stories, let me tell you. Treasure hunting had become a popular pastime on the land east of the pike, so much so that the owners had forbidden all trespassers. Not that it stopped anyone. Folks just started treasure hunting after dark. Every group that searched the hillside reported the same thing: They'd been frightened away by a ghost who was guarding the gold.

"I know of one group from Middlebrook that went treasure hunting," the bartender said as he refilled my glass. "They were digging around the hillside when a terrible windstorm came swooping down on them out of nowhere. The trees bent right down to the ground and the treasure hunters clung to every trunk and bush within reach to keep from blowing away. And the kicker? There wasn't a cloud in the sky to explain that wind! It was brought by the ghost. They all ran away and none of them will ever set foot on that hill again!"

The man on the barstool beside me remarked: "There was one fellow who was walking his girl home from church when they came face-to-face with the ghost on the pike. The fellow pulled out his gun, but his girl begged him not to shoot. The

THE PHANTOM OF MIDDLEBROOK PIKE

phantom drew so close the air turned ice cold and they reckoned it was going to grab one of them. But it just faded away."

More stories followed. A West End physician and a friend went ghost hunting to see if there was any truth to the rumors. When they reached the hillside where the purported treasure lay, a ghost sprang to life before their eyes. The physician took his horse whip and slashed at the phantom, but the whip went right through the glowing figure without touching it. The momentum threw him off-balance and he himself plummeted through the ghastly figure and fell to the ground. Afterward, he said it felt as if he had plunged through a slightly sticky snowbank. By the time his friend pulled him up, the spirit was gone.

A few lads from the woolen mills camped out at the haunted spot to "interview the ghost." About ten in the evening, a white mist rose from the root of a nearby tree and grew into a floating oblong block about six feet wide and one foot thick. The phantom gave a funny shake like a dog waking itself before it undulated in a circle. Then it slithered toward the watching lads like a giant snake. The boys opened fire with their guns, which shredded the misty oblong, but it snapped back together and kept coming. They watched in awe as it slid past them and disappeared among the trees.

"Some folks say it's really a white bear or maybe the Wampus Cat," the bartender said at the last call. "Others believe it's the old man guarding his gold. Who knows? The treasure hunters never found anything, but folks still like to ghost hunt on the Middlebrook Pike."

In the morning, I visited Benjamin's grave and did a quick reconnoiter of his former home. Now I was walking down

Middlebrook Pike, following the road my friend had frequented during his lifetime. I planned to spend the rest of the day comparing the local terrain to a roughly drawn map Benjamin had included with his letter.

The bartender and his buddies all agreed on the general vicinity of the haunting. They placed the ghost and his treasure on the east side of the pike. But every tree on the east side had been minutely examined and no treasure had been found. And Benjamin's map pointed me in a different direction. I strode into the woods on the west side of the pike. It took me about an hour of searching before I found a tree with a red-handled pocketknife thrust under one branch.

"Took you long enough," drawled Benjamin, stepping out from behind the tree. "What kept you?"

"Blame Susan," I said with a grin, holding out my hand to the phantom. Benjamin's handshake was firm but cold as ice. His skin was glowing slightly, but other than that he seemed the same. "I was out of town when the letter arrived, so she put it away for safekeeping. It took us years to find it."

Benjamin laughed. "I should have expected something like that to happen."

"It sounds like you've been having a heck of a good time scaring folks hereabouts," I said. "The bartender was telling me some stories."

"Sometimes it's me, sometimes it's the moonlight," said Benjamin, sitting down with his back to the tree. I sat down opposite and dropped my pack with a sigh.

"What about that windstorm? When did you learn to do that?" I asked.

"That wasn't me," Benjamin said, suddenly sober. "There's an old earth spirit that lives in these hills and it . . . she . . . doesn't like to be disturbed."

"Is that the Wampus Cat the bartender was talking about?" I asked curiously.

Benjamin frowned. "I've never liked that name. But yes, a native spirit from long ago. I lie low when she's in the area."

We sat chatting for nearly an hour, catching up on old times. It was good to see Benjamin again. I didn't bring up the hidden money. That wasn't what this trip was about. Finally, Benjamin sighed and stood up. "Well, you give Susan my best. I'll see you both in heaven, I expect. But not for a while yet. You stay here and spend time with those grandchildren of yours."

"I'll do that," I said.

We shook hands again and Benjamin vanished, just like that. When I picked up my pack, it was twice as heavy as before. I pocketed the red-handled knife and whistled as I made my way back to Middlebrook Pike.

"Thank you, Ben," I called as I stepped onto the road. "See you in heaven."

A puff of wind swirled around me. Then I was alone.

5

Barefoot Beauty

ROARING FORK

GREAT SMOKY MOUNTAINS NATIONAL PARK

I was feeling so terrible sad that I saddled up Red as soon as I finished my chores and took a ride beside the Roaring Fork. Usually, the sound of the water flowing over rocks soothes me, and the icy patterns made by the spray from the waterfalls was right pretty. But today, the sights and sounds of the Roaring Fork didn't raise my spirits the way I'd hoped.

I was heart sore on account of my gal Janie, who threw me over for a city fellow she met at a dance. I'd been courting Janie for many months and wanted her to wed with me, but she said we were through. The thought made me so miserable, I rode on and on through the snowy woods and didn't turn back at my usual spot.

It wasn't until the setting sun brought a chill breeze to the road that I came out of my sad thoughts and had a good look-round. I was plenty surprised when I realized where I was at. I tugged on the reins and said: "Whoa, Red. We'd best turn around. We're miles from home."

My body was shivering now that the sun was gone. I wanted a warm fire and a hot drink, but home was more than an hour

away in these icy conditions. I wasn't going to risk an injury to Red just because I'd been a durn fool about a girl. I decided right then that I was done thinking about Janie. "There's plenty more girls out there," I told Red as we headed back along the snowy road. My good old horse pricked his ears and snorted as if he agreed with me. I buttoned up my coat and wound my scarf over my nose and ears to keep them warm. It was going to be a chilly ride.

When we rounded a bend, I saw a slim figure walking along the cold snowy road. She wore a worn dress covered by a shawl that was too thin for such a cold night. And her feet were bare! My goodness, the girl would freeze to death if she lingered outside.

I called out and the girl turned to face at me and Red. She was so gosh durn pretty, she looked like a princess in a story book. Janie was driven clean out of my head. "Miss, you must be terrible cold," I exclaimed, pulling off my hat to be polite. "Can I give you a ride home?"

"That's right kind. Thank you," she said with a smile.

That smile done me in. My heart was banging so hard I thought she must be able to hear it. I slid down and swung her up into Red's saddle. Then I settled myself in front of her. Her thin arms slid around my waist and my body tingled from my head to my heels.

"Where do you live?" I asked.

She gave me directions to her house in a sweet voice that made me shiver with delight. As we rode toward her folks' place, she talked about how pretty the mountains were and how much she liked walking by the Roaring Fork. Just like me! She asked me about my family and what I did for work. I chattered away as if I'd always known her, which was unusual for a shy fellow like me.

Her house was the opposite direction from mine, but I didn't care. I could have ridden for days with that sweet girl behind me. It seemed like no time at all before we were riding into the little cove where her parents' cabin set.

I slid to the ground and swung her off the saddle. She was light as a feather and looking into her lovely eyes stole my breath away. "I forgot to ask yer name," I stammered, wanting to keep her with me as long as I could.

"Lucy," she said. "They call me Lucy."

"My name's F . . . foster," I returned.

She gave me a kiss on the cheek. "Thank you for the ride, Foster," she said.

I blushed a fiery red. I wanted to ask if I could call on her again, but she was already at the front door of the cabin. "Good night, Lucy," I called. She waved at me and stepped inside.

Behind me, Red gave a funny nicker and shook his head as if he were coming out of a daze. I didn't blame him. I felt that way myself.

All the way home, I dreamed about Lucy. I thought about her when I fed Red and put him away for the night. And when I cooked up a bachelor dinner for myself. And when I went to bed. And the next morning during chores. I was a wreck.

I held out for two days, and then I saddled up Red and headed out to Lucy's place to ask her folks if I could court her. It was a bright sunny day and melting snow made the whole world sound like a flowing stream. Spring was coming, and I would pick Lucy as many wildflowers as she could carry. And wed with her in the church as soon as she would let me.

BAREFOOT BEAUTY

When I rode into the cove where Lucy lived, her mama was working in the garden and her pa was chopping wood near the barn. They came over at once to ask my business.

I slid out of the saddle and took off my hat. "I met your daughter Lucy a couple days ago," I began, turning red. "She was walking home along the Roaring Fork. It was cold and her feet were bare, so I gave her a ride. We got to talking and we seemed to get along real nice, so I was wondering . . . that is, I'd like to court your daughter, if I may," I ended lamely.

Lucy's parents exchanged a look and her pa said: "What's your name, son?"

"My name is Foster," I replied.

"Foster, have a seat," he said, gesturing to a nearby stump. "I've got something to tell you, and it's best if you sit while I do."

I glanced at Lucy's ma and saw tears in her eyes. That alarmed me. Had something happened to Lucy?

I sat on the stump and faced Lucy's pa. He looked so sad that I braced myself. Was Lucy sick? Did I need to go for the doctor?

"There's no easy way to say this, son, so I'm just going to tell you. Lucy died in a cabin fire more than a year ago," her pa said heavily.

Lucy's ma started weeping softly into her apron.

"A year ago?" I asked, trying to make sense of what he said. Chills ran down my arms and legs. "Then who did I bring to your house the other night? She said she was Lucy."

"It was Lucy," said her pa. "Her ghost walks that road in the evenings. Roaring Fork was her favorite place to go when chores were done."

"I told you I heard the door open and close t'other night," Lucy's ma said through her tears. "I knew it was Lucy, come for a visit."

I was feeling poorly. My stomach heaved and my head felt dizzy. That beautiful girl was a ha'nt? How could that be? All my plans for the future were ruined in just a few words.

Lucy's pa grabbed my shoulder and steadied me so I wouldn't fall off the stump.

"I'm sorry, son. I'm glad she liked you. She would have been happy to be courted by a gentleman such as yourself."

Lucy's ma fetched me some water to drink and showed me a picture of her daughter. I stared into the lovely face, just like a storybook princess. I handed the picture back with trembling hands.

"Thank you for telling me," I said.

I stood up stiffly, feeling like an old man, and climbed slowly into the saddle. Lucy's folks nodded their farewell. Her ma was crying again.

I walked Red out of the clearing and then set him galloping down the wet roadway as fast as we could go. I was sad and scared half to death and angry. First Janie and now Lucy. I had the worse luck with women.

"Looks like you and me are bachelors again, Red," I told my horse when we slowed to a walk. "I'm done with courting. At least for now!"

6

The Ghost Club

ASHEVILLE, NORTH CAROLINA

It all started with the newspaper article. Nathaniel was reading in his usual spot on the steps of the schoolhouse while the rest of us threw a ball around the yard after lunch. Nathaniel's pa was a big man in the railroad business. He traveled a lot and brought home newspapers from everywhere he went for his intellectual son. Nathaniel faithfully read them during the lunch hour while the rest of us were relaxing.

The girls were gathered in their usual group, talking and laughing. Mary kept catching my eye, and whenever she did, I dropped the ball and the other fellows jeered at me. I flushed and vowed to keep my eye on the ball, but then Mary looked at me again and I never even noticed it flying over my head.

Before I could retrieve the ball, a bellow interrupted our sport.

"Fellows!" Nathaniel shouted. He was waving his father's old newspaper over his head like a wild man as he ran toward us. "Fellows! Look at this article about Crawfordsville, Indiana."

"Why should we care about Crawfordsville, Indiana?" one fellow asked.

"Because they have a Ghost Club," Nathaniel said excitedly.

That got our attention. Everyone—even the girls—hurried over to see his newspaper. It was a long article, so Nathaniel summed it up for us. Apparently, a group in Crawfordsville had formed a club whose membership had one single requirement: The members must have personally seen a ghost at least once in their lives. The club was formed on October 31—All Hallows' Eve—and each year they indoctrinated new members. They met regularly to tell true ghost stories in a building that itself had several hauntings. Several of their ghostly tales were related in the article, but before we could read any of them, Nathaniel folded the paper under his arms and said: "I think we should do it!"

"Do what?" asked a girl suspiciously.

"I think we should form our own Society For Advancement of Belief in Ghosts," Nathaniel said patiently.

"How can we? We've never seen a ghost," a boy pointed out skeptically.

"I have," said Nathaniel promptly. "My granny is Scottish and I was born with her sixth sense."

"I have too," I said at once. Well, it was probably a sheet flapping on a windy night, but since I never went to check before running for the house, I figure it could have been a ghost.

"I live in a haunted house," Mary volunteered. "My father's sister fell down the staircase the night before her wedding and broke her neck. Her ghost is said to haunt the staircase and the front parlor."

The schoolyard was suddenly filled with scholars vying to tell their personal ghost stories. Alas, the bell rang at that moment and we were called back to class. But not before a bunch of us agreed to meet after school to discuss the Ghost Club. The upshot of that meeting was the inauguration of the Asheville Ghost Club on All Hallows' Eve, which was a week away.

Mary's parents were spiritualists and were happy to host our first club meeting in their haunted home. The whole family pitched in to turn their front parlor into a spooky masterpiece that rivaled the description in Nathaniel's newspaper. On All Hallows' Eve, every member of our class showed up on Mary's doorstep at the appointed hour; even Gregory who claimed he'd spent a night in a haunted graveyard in order to qualify for the club. His tale of a misty figure rising from a grave was probably as real as my haunted sheet, but there was no way either of us were missing out on this club.

Mary looked pretty as a picture standing in the doorway greeting all her classmates. She blushed when I complemented her dress and fluttered her eyelashes when she told me she'd saved me a seat. She ushered us into the parlor, which was deliciously creepy. White cheesecloth hung from the ceiling and draped the walls. The posh furnishings had been replaced with rows of chairs covered in black cloth which faced a massive table that stood in front of the fireplace. On the table lay a bell, a prayer book, and a candle to lay any ghosts that were raised that night, in accordance with the tenets of ghost lore. There were skeletons in each corner with red lanterns lighting up the mouth and eye sockets in a suitably gruesome manner.

The spooky atmosphere within the shadowy room gave me goose bumps. Or maybe it was the presence of Mary by my side. Her parents welcomed us to their home before retiring to the dining room to chaperone from a discreet distance.

Nathaniel took his place behind the table. We had already elected him club president, so he brought us to order and explained the rules drawn up for our club and the meeting schedule. He'd even written out a charter for us to sign.

After the formalities were concluded, we took a short break before regrouping for the main event. According to our new club rules, there would be two formal presentations per meeting. Each speaker would tell a true ghost story that they themselves had experienced. After the stories were concluded, they would answer questions and we would have a group discussion before closing with cake and refreshments. Nathaniel and Mary had volunteered to be the first two presenters.

Nathaniel resumed his place behind the table and began his ghost story. "When I was seven, my parents took me to a box supper at the church. It was a lovely evening, so we decided to walk since the sanctuary wasn't far from our house. The church was packed with families and there were lots of children my age running around having a great time."

Nathaniel paused for a sip of water, then continued. "At first, I didn't notice the barefoot little girl in the white dress. She was much younger than me—maybe four or five—and she wasn't from any of the families with which we were acquainted. She started following me as I went from table to table to talk with my friends. And she followed me outside when a bunch of us wanted to run races to get out all the energy from all the pies and cakes we'd eaten. She watched so wistfully that I considered asking her to play with us. But my buddies thought girls were nuisances and wouldn't have been polite. So I ignored her, hoping she'd go back to her family or find some girls to play with."

Nathaniel tugged on his fingers as if he still felt guilty for ignoring the little girl. "It was getting dark, so my parents

THE GHOST CLUB

gathered our things and we said good night to our friends. By the time we left the church, I had forgotten all about the barefoot little girl in white. It was only when we turned onto the road that led to our home that I saw her shyly following us. I stopped and pointed sternly back to the church. 'Go back to your family, little girl. They will be missing you,' I said. My parents turned to look at me. 'Who are you talking to, Nathaniel?' asked my mother. I pointed toward the little girl, who was standing a couple feet away. She watched us with interest and gave no sign of wanting to leave. 'I'm talking to that little girl. She followed me around during the box supper and she won't go back to the church. Her parents will be worried.'"

Nathaniel took another swallow of water. His face was several shades paler than normal and the paper from which he was reading shook in his hands. "My father frowned and said: 'I do not see anyone standing there, Nathaniel.' And suddenly, neither did I."

Everyone in the room gasped.

"The barefoot little girl had vanished without a trace. I'd been followed all evening by a ghost," Nathaniel confirmed our suspicions. "I gasped and started shaking all over with fright. My parents, to their credit, believed my story at once. They took me home and put me to bed with a glass of warm milk. My father went back to the church to ask if anyone knew about the ghost of a little girl that haunted the place. The pastor told him that a little girl fitting his description had been killed in a carriage accident in front of the sanctuary.

"She was buried in the churchyard. Her parents moved away from Asheville, but her cousins still lived in town and claimed that they often saw the little girl in the churchyard, watching other children play."

We clapped vigorously at the conclusion of Nathaniel's tale, but our enthusiasm did little to dispel the gloomy menace that enveloped the room. The red light emanating from the skull's eye sockets flickered, making the shadows around us dance. The air felt so cold, I expected ice crystals to form in front of my nose each time I breathed out.

When the clapping ceased, a pale young woman stepped to the front of the room. She was wearing a long white gown that nearly blended with the cheesecloth hanging around the room. Her presence seemed to cast a spell over the room. She was unknown to us, but we did not question her appearance. Indeed, we were all mesmerized as she told her tale.

"It was an arranged marriage," the woman began. "Two prominent local families decided to unite their lineage. The son of a penniless nobleman was marrying the eldest daughter of a rich merchant. Thus the middleclass family gained prestige and the nobleman's family procured a fortune."

The pale woman's voice was sibilant and strange. Icy chills were running up and down my spine. Mary's clasp on my hand grew so tight I lost the sensation in my fingers.

"The merchant's daughter loved the noble heir. He was darkly handsome with flashing eyes and a roguish grin. His courtship was dashing and outwardly sincere. He brought her flowers and expensive gifts. He wooed her with pretty words. Everything on the surface seemed perfect and a grand wedding was planned. But something was not right. The girl's brother was concerned. The heir had been seen several times around town, flirting with the daughter of a lawyer who had just moved to Asheville."

The pale woman paused. The room was so still you could hear the wind whistling outside the window. It was a lonely sound.

"The wedding invitations were sent, the wedding gown purchased, the paperwork uniting the family fortunes signed. There was no backing out of the marriage, no matter how many lawyer's daughters moved to town," the pale woman said. "In spite of her brother's concern, the merchant's daughter was hopeful. She was a beautiful girl herself and she was sure the heir noble loved her. To ease her brother's mind, she sent a note to the heir asking him to meet her at the house. It was the eve of her wedding and therefore unlucky for the groom to see his bride. Knowing the family would object to this lapse in tradition, she asked the heir to meet her upstairs in a private sitting room where they could talk without being disturbed. There, the merchant's daughter asked the heir about the other woman. The heir's eyes flashed with anger at her words, and the truth spilled out. He did not love her. He had never loved her. If it weren't for the money, he would never marry her."

An indignant rustle passed through the room. The pale woman waited until it subsided to continue.

"The heir stormed out of the room and the merchant's daughter followed, threatening to break their engagement and nullify the agreement between their families. The heir and the merchant's daughter stood face-to-face at the top of the staircase, glaring at each other. Then a cruel smile crossed the heir's face. 'You will never break our engagement,' he told the merchant's daughter and pushed her down the stairs. When she lay crumpled and broken at the bottom, the heir slipped away unnoticed. No one ever knew he had been in the house the night the merchant's daughter died."

Someone gasped and we all turned to see Mary's father standing in the doorway of the dining room. "Maud?" he whispered, staring in disbelief at the pale woman. "Maud, is that true? Did Henry kill you?"

My eyes widened as his words registered in my mind. I stared in shock as I realized that the pale woman standing beside the massive table was a ghost.

"Henry pushed me down the stairs on the eve of our wedding," Maud's spirit confirmed. "There was a clause in the marriage agreement that said the money would go to the heir if I died before the wedding, provided the engagement was not broken. When I threatened to end our betrothal, Henry knew the only way to keep the money was to kill me. So that is what he did."

"The scoundrel. The reprobate!" Mary's father was incoherent with rage.

"Tell our father the truth," Maud said. "That is all I ask." Her pale body grew translucent and then faded slowly away.

There was a moment of stunned silence. Then my classmates screamed and a mass exodus ensued. Within moments, there was not a soul left in the room save Mary, her father, and me.

Mary's father sank into a black-draped chair. He was trembling from head to toe.

"What will you do, sir?" I asked, since Mary seemed incapable of speech.

"I will tell my father the truth," Mary's father said. "There's nothing we can do about the marriage agreement. Without proof of the murder, it is impossible to break. It is our word against Henry's.

And it happened so many years ago that Henry and his family are long returned to England." He rubbed a trembling hand over his face, looking lost and sorrowful.

"I think Aunt Maud just wanted us to know the truth," Mary said, hurrying over to hug her father.

I helped the family clean up the front parlor before taking my leave. Mary walked me to the front door.

"Well, no one will ever forget the first meeting of the Ghost Club," I said as stepped out into the chilly air of All Hallows' Eve.

"Do you think there will be a second meeting?" she asked dryly.

"Heavens, I hope not," I said sincerely. "I don't need any more convincing. Aunt Maud's ghost was as real as they come."

The next day at school, Nathaniel tore up the charter and we unanimously agreed that the gathering on All Hallows' Eve was the first and only meeting of the Asheville Ghost Club. Rest in peace, Aunt Maud.

7

There's Two of Them Tonight

CADES COVE

GREAT SMOKY MOUNTAINS NATIONAL PARK

We were a bunch of pesky young 'uns back in those days, living deep in the woods, going to school in Cades Cove, and attending church on a Sunday. After schooling and chores were done, we'd head down to the creek to relax and dare each other to do stupid things. It was the dares that led me into a mess of trouble with a ha'nt one night.

It started at the corn-husking party. A local family placed a huge pile of corn in the middle of their yard with a half-gallon of moonshine hidden beneath it and invited all the neighbors to help them with the shucking. Everyone in the community showed up for the event. Folks brought their very best dishes to share at the evening meal and several fellows brought their instruments, so there'd be music and dancing after the moonshine was found.

There were two corn-shucking teams trying to beat one another to the whiskey, but our little group wasn't much help. Most of us fellers were sparking one or another of the local girls, and we figured this was a good time to impress them. My buddy decided we should scare the girls with some ha'nt stories, so we took turns telling our best tales. I sat next my sweetheart, hoping to get a red ear of corn so I could kiss her. When it was my turn, I told her my very best ha'nt story, hoping she'd be so skeered she'd cuddle up close.

"There was once a feller who married a Cades Cove girl who was born during a thunderstorm," I began. Everyone huddled close so as not to miss a word. "Now everyone knows if'n you were born during a thunderstorm; you'll be killed by lightening. Well, this girl didn't want to die, so she refused to sleep in a metal bed. She was a champion quilter, but she wouldn't even use a metal sewing needle if'n there was a storm brewing."

My sweetheart nodded at her thoughtfully as she started shucking another ear of corn. "That was right smart of her," she said.

"Now this girl made her husband a quilt using pieces from a red shirt he wore during their first big argument," I continued. "She called it the cussing quilt and it was one of the finest she ever made. One day, she got real sick and even the doctor couldn't save her. On her death bed, she made her husband promise two things: He had to keep her quilts in the family, and her quilts should never be put on a metal bed."

I paused to pick up another ear of corn before continuing the story. "The feller gave his solemn promise, but he didn't keep it. When he brought a new wife home, she insisted on using a metal frame for their bed. The first night it got cold, the new wife got out the cussing quilt, and she put it on that metal bed. Around midnight, the new wife woke up all a-shiver and saw a ghost hovering over her. It was the feller's first wife.

Suddenly, a bolt of lightning smashed down into the bedroom. The new wife was knocked clean out of her senses. When she came to, she found her husband's body lying on the floor. He'd been charred to a cinder by that lightning bolt and the metal bed was nothing but a pile of ashes. But there wasn't a scorch mark on the cussing quilt. And you know what else was strange? There weren't any thunderstorms in Cades Cove that evening."

The girls shivered and exclaimed, while the boys exchanged triumphant glances. The girls would be sticking close to us fellers the rest of the evening to keep the ha'nts away.

Then one of the girls asked: "Any of you boys ever seen a ha'nt?"

I wanted to say "yes" to impress my sweetheart. But everyone would know I was lying. I shook my head, and so did the rest of the boys.

"I heard the cemetery is ha'nted," a beauty called Betty said. "My brother says at midnight, a ghost sits on the big headstone and tries to grab anyone who walks past. He's seen it himself."

"I'd like to see that," my sweetheart said with a sideways glance at me. "If'n you're brave enough to take me there at midnight."

"Is that a dare?" I asked boldly, giving her a wink.

"I dare you," she said, flushing pink.

That settled that. There was no way I was going to say no, even though I knew Ma and Pa would go through the roof if they found out I snuck out at midnight to look for ha'nts.

We made plans to meet the girls at our favorite spot just before midnight, and we'd walk together to the cemetery.

"What if the ha'nt don't show?" asked my best buddy.

THERE'S TWO OF THEM TONIGHT

"We best make sure a ha'nt does show, or the girls won't speak to us again," I said.

I should have kept my big mouth shut. But I didn't, and that's how I came to be shivering on top of a cold tombstone in an empty graveyard at midnight with a white sheet over my head while my buddies walked the girls to the cemetery. I felt kind of bad for fooling the girls into believing I was a ha'nt, but the other fellers said it was for the best. The girls would scream and run away. Then I would come a-running up behind the group, pretending I was late, and they'd tell me all about it. Maybe I'd lose a few points with my girl for missing the ha'nt, but I could make it up by taking her to the social later this month.

The tombstone was so chilly that the cold seeped through my trousers, making me shiver under my sheet. The wind whipped the treetops so they bent and whispered and moaned. It was real creepy. Every owl hoot or grass rustle made me jump. Where was everyone? I didn't like being alone in this here cemetery, plus my rear was getting so numb I like to die of frostbite if I had to keep setting on this tomb.

Then I heard my sweetheart's voice drifting down the road. She said: "It's not like Jake to be late. He's going to miss the ha'nt."

The group was walking up the road with nary a light between 'em. They didn't want to scare off the ha'nt before they'd seen it. They were getting closer and closer to the cemetery. Time for my big act!

I scrambled to my knees atop that tombstone and spread my arms wide in my best ha'nt imitation. I'd give the girls something to remember!

A moment later, Betty shrieked: "Lord Almighty! There's two of them tonight!"

Two of them?

I turned my head. A glowing white figure floated beside my tombstone. It was right next to my arm, and it was so cold that it felt like someone was stabbing icicles under my skin. Two eyes glowed into mine, and it opened its mouth into a grin that was too wide to be normal. I could see its teeth and a glowing tongue. I thought it was going to bite my head off!

I screamed and shot off that tombstone like a ball out of a cannon. I wasn't the only one shouting. The girls were wailing as the boys were dragging them down the road as fast as they could run.

The ha'nt made a grab for me on the way down from the tombstone, but it missed. Or maybe it didn't miss, 'cause it felt like more icicles were passing through my arms and chest. Thank the Almighty, the ghost was only partially there. If it manifested fully, I might have been dragged down into the grave with it.

I forgot about my sheet until it whipped off me and dropped into the dirt. I had to go back for it. Ma would kill me if she found it was missing. When I turned back, the road behind me was empty. I guess the ha'nt was tied to the cemetery somehow. Or maybe it didn't think I was worth chasing.

I folded up the sheet with trembling hands, then I went to find my friends.

My sweetheart hugged me around the neck, a-sobbing about the ha'nt. She weren't worried for herself. Turns out, she was skeered I'd gotten to the cemetery before the rest of them and the ha'nt had grabbed me.

"We will never visit the cemetery at midnight, ever again," she said, wiping away the last of her tears. "You promise me Jake. Never again."

I was never so happy to make a promise in my whole life. And unlike the feller with the cussing cover, I intended to keep it.

8

Matchmaking Ghost

It was the year of our Lord 1875 and I was a successful young man living and working in Knoxville. But business drew me to a remote town in the Smoky Mountains region of Blount County. I was staying at the house of one Mr. Rubert, who had a son, Austin, who was twenty years old—the same age as myself—and quite the intellectual. The house was also occupied by my hostess, the delightful Mrs. Rubert and by two charming daughters: Adela, who was seventeen, and her sister Julia, who was fifteen. The girls were pretty as posies, and I could not choose between them. Adela was sweet-tempered and kind. Julia was full of spice and her wit made me laugh until my sides ached.

By the close of my visit, the Rubert siblings and I were talking and laughing as if we'd known one another for years. On my last evening, we were sitting by the fire playing silly word games when a loud crash interrupted our chatter. It sounded as if a large building were falling down. A loud scream tore through the chilly night air.

I rushed to the front door, most of the Rubert family upon my heels. Only the fair young Julia remained calm. "I don't know what you are fussed about," she called from her cozy place by the fire. "It is only Bill Jenkins, running from the ghost again."

She had scarcely finished her sentence when a wiry fellow came bursting out of the shadowy darkness, blowing like a steam engine. He pushed through the crowded doorway and collapsed into the first available chair.

"Whatever is the matter, Bill?" Mr. Rubert demanded as I studied this new addition to our party. Dark haired with the straggly beginnings of a beard, his face was deathly pale and his whole frame shook. His eyes rolled hither and yon, searching the corners of the snug house for unknown terrors.

"Out there! Yonder. It was a ha'nt most terrible," Bill stammered. "It was moaning and groaning and snuffling in the shadows. And there was a wee phantom baby crying 'til it broke yer heart to hear it."

This strapping fellow was scared of ghosts? I burst out laughing. "You must be joking," I gasped between gusts of merriment.

"T'aint no laughing matter," Bill said solemnly. "The ha'nts is very real. I'll swear on a stack of Bibles if'n you don't believe me."

I turned to my friend Austin. "Tell you what, old boy. Let us walk Bill back to the place where he heard the noises and solve this ghost matter for him."

To my surprise, Austin avoided my gaze, and I realized that he was frightened.

"Darn me to heck, pardon ladies, but I ain't going back there," said Bill.

"It doesn't look like Austin is going either," said Adela, eyeing her brother in concern.

"You aren't superstitious, are you, old man?" I asked incredulously.

"Of course not," Austin said a shade too quickly. "I am just afraid of catching cold. There will be a frost tonight."

"What nonsense," Julia said, rising from her seat by the fire. "Let us all go. Mr. Marion, Austin, Adela, and myself. There is a full moon tonight and it will make a pleasant walk before bedtime. Bill, will you come?"

"Not I," gasped the wiry Bill Jenkins. "I've had enough ha'nts fer one evening, thank ya kindly Miss Julia."

After ascertaining the place where Bill Jenkins had heard the ghosts, the four of us set out. We soon found the source of the crash. Bill had knocked over some twenty panels of the Ruberts' fence in his panic.

Another two hundred paces or so down the road, we came to a dark hollow where the timber was tall and thick. Nary a glimmer of moonlight made its way through the dense cover overhead. The wind rustled the leaves and rattled through the underbrush, sending shivers down my spine. You could easily believe that something dark and menacing lay in the shadowy woods around us. Our merry conversation faltered in this spooky place, and Austin nearly jumped out of his skin when a grunting, snuffling sound erupted from the bushes beside him.

"Ou-woo-boo-hoo-ugh-ugh," something groaned in the shrubbery.

Austin howled and jumped back, clutching at Adela, who emitted tiny shrieks of fear. In vivid contrast to her siblings, the intrepid Julia glided to my side and said: "This must be Bill's ghost."

"Onward, then," I said, setting aside my own jitters in favor of scientific discovery. I advanced into the darkness, the fair Julia on my heels.

"Ou-woo-boo-hoo-ugh-ugh," the spirit groaned again, almost at my elbow.

I looked down upon the shadowy form of a hog curled up on the side of the road. It was muttering in its sleep, twisting this way and that to get comfortable. I burst out laughing once again.

"What is it?" asked Austin, creeping up behind me.

Before I could respond, the rest of the herd woke and made a mass exit, squealing and squawling as badly as Bill had a few minutes before.

Austin was sheepish the whole journey back. "Hogs," he kept muttering. "It was just hogs!"

But Bill Jenkins wasn't so sure when we reported our find. "I know the difference between a ha'nt and a hog," he insisted. "Them hogs musta come up after I did."

He went home in a bit of a huff and the rest of us settled again by the fire.

"You must not blame Bill," Adela said, looking up from her knitting. "That hollow has always had a reputation for being haunted. Tell Mr. Marion about the ghost and John Kinsler, Julia. You tell that story best."

Julia took a sip of apple cider, and then told the following tale.

A young man named John Kinsler was passing down the road one dark night in autumn a little over a year ago. As he reached the dark hollow, he saw a glimmer of white rise up before him. It was the spirit of a long-deceased woman. John Kinsler froze in place, not knowing if he should pray or run.

Before he could do either, the spirit raised her arms and said: "John Kinsler. John Kinsler! If you will be happy, you must marry Jane Merton and have the Rubert family at the wedding. Remember this, John Kinsler!" With a final moan, the spirit dropped her arms and ascended slowly upward into the trees until she vanished from view.

John Kinsler uttered a shriek of terror and ran back home on legs that shook like saplings in a wind storm. But he took that spirit's message to heart and married Jane Merton before the month was out. And the Rupert family were the first ones invited to the wedding. John Kinsler wasn't taking any chances with this message from the other side.

"You make the whole thing sound dashed convincing," I remarked when Julia finished her story. "I think I would like to see a ghost. A real one, I mean. Not just a herd of hogs."

"Maybe you will one day," Julia said.

But Austin told me I'd come to regret that wish one day and turned the conversation.

I thought about the spooky hollow and the hogs that night in bed. It still made me chuckle to myself. I really didn't believe in ghosts. I also spared a thought for the sweet Adela and the spunky Julia. They were pretty as a picture, the two of them, and I thought it a pity that I had to return to Knoxville in the morning. It would have been nice to know them better.

Two years had passed in the blink of an eye, and I found myself once again passing through Blount County on business. I called on my friend Mr. Rubert, who was very pleased to renew our acquaintance. When he learned I was in town for a prolonged period, he insisted I stay with his family. "You will be much more comfortable with us," he told me repeatedly.

MATCHMAKING GHOST

Things had changed quite a bit since my last visit. Austin was married and the fair Adela was engaged to a promising young attorney. Julia was still serving sauce, as they say, and was even prettier than I remembered. I figured it would not be long before she too was betrothed. She probably had a string of fellows on her line already, I thought, and wondered why the notion made me feel melancholy.

Talk of the haunted hollow drove such thoughts out of my head. The reputation of the place had grown over the years. Locals had encountered everything from angels to the devil himself in that locale, and more than one match was credited to the moaning woman of the hollow.

Scientific curiosity aroused, I was anxious to encounter one of these spirits for myself. During my stay, I passed through the haunted hollow at every possible time of day and night, but I felt not a frisson of foreboding, nor heard I a sound that did not belong.

"Perhaps I do not have the right kind of mind to see a spirit," I said to Adela and Julia one night over dinner. "The gift seems to have evaded me."

"The spirit may be biding its time," Adela said comfortingly. Her attitude toward the haunted hollow had shifted dramatically since the moaning woman of the hollow had made her a match. Mrs. Rubert told me the story in confidence the first evening of my stay. Apparently, Adela's beau was inspiring in the courtroom and desperately shy everywhere else. The family thought he would never get up the nerve to propose to their daughter, and Adela was growing thin from weeping herself to sleep at night in despair. But the Ruberts had reckoned without the ghost. One night after seeing Adela home from a church social, the attorney had encountered the moaning woman in the hollow. The spirit lit into him something awful for breaking Adela's heart and the man ran home screaming in fear. He came back at dawn the next day and proposed to Adela, and they were to be wed next month.

I was late coming home the following evening, and my mind was on business when I entered the haunted hollow. It was a complete shock when a white figure rose suddenly in front of me. I froze in my tracks, heart pounding so hard it hurt. I held my breath, waiting for the ghost to speak. It looked like the figure they called the moaning woman, but that was all I could make out in the darkness. Should I speak to it? I couldn't decide.

Then the phantom stretched its white arms toward me and moaned: "Marion. Mr. Mariooooon!"

Shivers ran down my arms and legs. I felt wobbly and had to clench my knees to keep from falling over.

"Mr. Marion," the ghost moaned again. "If you would be happy, you must marry Julia Rubert. Remember, Mr. Mariooooon!"

The figure raised its arms above its head and ascended from the earth. A moment later, it vanished into the treetops.

I gasped several times, slamming my fist against my chest to help me breathe. I had wanted to see a spirit, and now I had. But I'd be thrice blasted to heck if I ran like Bill Jenkins.

I waited until my trembling ceased before making my way to the Ruberts' home. As I stepped out of the haunted hollow, I heard a roaring sound behind me. I did not look back. One spirit was enough for me. The roaring phantom would have to wait for another victim.

I went to bed early that night, not wanting to encounter Adela or her sister. I refused to think about the ghost's message. I'd be darned if I'd let a ghost choose a wife for me. Even one as fair and lively as Julia Rubert.

When I stepped into the parlor the next morning, I found Julia sitting alone by the fireplace. She blushed when she saw me and looked away. I felt rather flushed myself. I looked around to make sure no one else was present and then told Julia that I'd finally seen the ghost for myself. I did not mention its supernatural message. That part was private.

Julia turned bright pink and confessed that she too had seen a phantom a few days prior to my haunting. "Are you superstitious now?" she asked with a spark of her old spirit.

"Of course not," I said with some bravado. I don't think she believed me. "I will keep investigating this spirit. Surely there is a scientific explanation for it. Would you give me your word that you will not mention my encounter with the phantom?"

Julia promised to keep silent.

For the next two weeks, I walked home through the haunted hollow each night, determined to see the phantom once again. I was determined to ask it some hard questions during our next encounter. Ghosts were supposed to answer when you spoke to them. At least, that's what I'd read in the newspaper. To my dismay, the moaning woman did not return to the hollow.

I was sorely disappointed and complained freely to Julia about it. She did not seem as sympathetic as previously. I wondered what had put her out of sorts.

On the evening before my departure, I went for one last walk in the haunted hollow. Maybe, if I was lucky, I'd see the ghost again and ask it my questions. Or rather, one burning question that kept creeping into my mind whenever I saw Julia bent over a book or doing her needlework in the firelight.

I was thinking so hard about Julia that at first, I didn't notice the white figure standing about twenty paces from me. It hovered in the same place as before. My heart started pounding, but this time it was excitement, not fear that sent it racing in response. Now I could ask it my question. But before I could open my mouth, the figure howled: "Marioooon! Mr. Marion! Tomorrow you leave this place! And you have not asked Julia Rubert to be your wife. Go and ask her at once. Remember, Marion!"

The phantom lifted its arms toward the treetops and started to rise.

"Oh no you don't! Not until I've asked you my question," I roared and leapt forward. I grabbed the white figure in my arms. I wasn't expecting to catch anything, but to my surprise, my hands closed around solid flesh. The figure gave a shriek of rage as we ascended together toward the treetops. I was pretty sure I could feel a rope looped about the ghost's hands and feet.

"Let me down," I shouted at the ghost.

"If I return you to the earth, you must leave this place immediately," the spirit moaned.

"I'll promise anything to get down from here," I said.

"Then let us go down," the spirit shouted loudly. It sounded as if it was giving instructions to an invisible companion.

Down we went. As soon as we touched the ground, I whipped out my knife and cut the rope over the spirit's head. The phantom shrieked and fell to the ground, shouting: "You dare disturb me? Beware, for Beelzebub the king of demons approaches!"

When the ghost tried to run away, I grabbed hold and wouldn't let go. When a massive figure draped in black came striding toward us, I snatched up a stick with my free hand and brandished it. The demonic form hesitated long enough for me to sweep up the ghost and take off at a run for the Ruberts' place. In my haste, I nearly knocked over the fence in the same manner as Bill Jenkins two years prior.

I burst into the parlor and shoved the phantom into the chair, shouting for a light. The whole household tumbled into the room, as I unmasked the ghost. Moments later, a sheepish Julia Rupert was revealed as the phantom. When our eyes met, she burst into remorseful tears. So overcome was she that her mother and Adela took her to her room.

"I don't understand," poor Mr. Rubert exclaimed.

"It's nothing to be concerned about, sir" I said, pouring him a stiff drink. "Just a small prank played by your high-spirited daughter. She knew I was looking for ghosts and so she provided me with one."

I made no mention of either of the girls' messages to me. Those were private.

When Mr. Rubert finally excused himself, I wandered outside and went to confront the second member of this supernatural committee. I found the Ruberts' hired man in his little cottage. Old Sam gave me a sheepish smile when he saw me.

"You are Beelzebub, I presume?" I asked lightly.

"You figured it out," Old Sam said with a grin. "I told Miss Julia you were a smart 'un. If'n anybody could figure it out, it'd be you. We've been playing ghost pranks on folks for years, ever since Miss Julia was a young 'un. She's made matches for most of the young ladies in this community. Guess she thought it was her turn."

We eyed one another while I considered his words. So Julia Rubert had been courting me all along. It was an unconventional wooing, but there was nothing conventional about Julia Rubert. I knew a rare treasure when I met one. Julia was a woman of spirit, intelligence, laughter, and courage. If this was her way of winning me, then so be it. I wasn't going to disappoint her hopes.

My thoughts must have shown on my face, for Old Sam beamed with delight and jumped up to shake my hand.

"No more pranks," I told him. "The phantom and Beelzebub need to stand down!"

"Yessir!" Old Sam said.

Julia and I were married six months later. She made a beautiful bride and a fine wife. A boy and a girl soon joined our family, which added to our happiness. Never once in all our years of my marriage did I regret meeting the moaning woman in the hollow or taking her excellent matchmaking advice.

9

The Watcher

Joe had timed his backpacking trip along this portion of the Appalachian Trail so that he could see the dawn from the top of Clingmans Dome. It had been a bit brutal, getting up so early and hiking in the dark. But he was in luck and it was a clear day, so it was worth the sacrifice of a little sleep.

Joe had been raised in the foothills of the Smoky Mountains and returned whenever he could to hike and fish. His job had taken him far away from these hills, but this was his heart's home, and always would be.

Joe avoided the lookout tower at the top of Clingmans Dome and found his favorite gap in the trees. There was a rock where he liked to perch and watch the sunrise. He set down his gear, gulped water, and stared out over the misty mountaintops, east toward the spot where the sun would shortly rise. The clouds were already turning pink and gold. He heard a hawk call and when he turned his head to follow its flight, he caught a glimpse of a Cherokee man sitting on a stump nearby. Joe jumped and water from his bottle splashed his shirt. He hadn't noticed anyone when he arrived at this private lookout.

THE WATCHER

The man wore traditional garb, which surprised Joe. He had many friends among the Cherokee, and most of them dressed like him. But there could be some private ceremony scheduled for today, or the man might be on a spiritual quest. Joe didn't think it would be polite to ask. Instead, he apologized for disturbing the man's peace and stood up. He could watch the dawn from another spot.

"You are not disturbing me," the man said mildly. "Stay and watch the sunrise with me."

Joe thanked him and settled back onto his rock. The two men sat in silence as the birds welcomed the new day and little creatures came out from their holes and burrows to eat. The light grew stronger, the colors on the horizon intensified. There was a dream-like quality in the air, and when the old Cherokee spoke into this sacred moment, his words burning themselves into Joe's memory for all time.

I remember when my people were forced to leave. I was living in a small cabin with my wife and sons and knew nothing of the politics raging in Washington, for I was far more concerned with the weather and my crops than with the actions of people who lived far away from my hills. Until the day my brother-in-law came to tell us that companies of soldiers were searching the valleys of our home and herding thousands of Cherokee people into stockades in preparation for a great march to the west. It seemed fantastical to me, but my brother-in-law was an honest man, and I knew it must be so.

I returned to my work with a heavy heart, wondering what the future would bring. And then I had a vision. I saw my people living and working, laughing, and crying and playing in these mountains many years into the future. They would be born here, wed here, die here, and would carry on the traditions and wisdom passed to us from our ancestors. I paused, stunned by this dream that had come to my mind. Was it possible? Could we resist this removal and win?

White soldiers came to our cabin and ordered us to join the other Cherokee in the stockade at Bushnell. We were given little time to prepare and could take only the belongings we could carry. Outwardly, I was calm but inwardly, I was furious. How dare they force us off our land? I had signed no treaty. I had not even known there was a treaty until my brother-in-law had arrived.

The soldiers marched us away from our home with little sympathy for our plight. When my dear wife stumbled in fatigue, one of the soldiers prodded her cruelly with his bayonet. Enraged, I spoke to my kinsmen in Cherokee: "When we reach the turn in the trail, I will trip and fall and complain of my ankle. When the soldiers stop, take their guns. We'll escape into the hills."

At the appropriate moment, I collapsed onto the path and my sons leapt upon their captors with the help of my brother-in-law. In the fight that followed, one of the soldiers was killed. We fled, knowing the fury of the white men would follow us.

I led my family up into the mountains to a concealed cave under the peak known as Clingmans Dome. We lived as fugitives through the long summer that followed, foraging as best we could and avoiding the soldiers who hunted us.

The Watcher

After the last band of Cherokee departed in the autumn, Will Thomas, a white trader who had been adopted by a Cherokee chief, came to our cave on Clingmans Dome. He told us about the other Cherokee—numbering about a thousand—who had taken refuge in the mountains. Then he relayed a message from the US General Scott: "If Tsali and his kin will come in and give up, I won't hunt down the others. If Tsali will voluntarily pay the penalty, I will intercede with the government to grant the fugitives permission to remain. But if Tsali refuses, I'll turn my soldiers loose to hunt every one of them."

I sat in silence, considering the general's words. In my mind I saw again the vision I had in the field: my people living and working, laughing and loving and dying in these mountains as they carried on the traditions and wisdom passed to us from our ancestors. As I looked at the faces of my family, I saw the same determination in each face. If our deaths could bring about such a future, how could we say no?

When we left our hiding place, we were met by a band of the Oconaluftee Cherokee who lived in Quallatown, those for whom our sacrifice would be made. They brought us to the stockade and our trial was swiftly over. My elder son, my brother-in-law, and I were sentenced to die, but my wife and youngest son were spared. We were taken to the field next to the stockade and stood against the trees. The colonel in charge asked us for our final words, and I asked if we could be shot by our own people. They acceded to my request and three Cherokee men were selected to be our executioners. I saw in their faces that they understood the sacrifice we were making on their behalf. We waved aside the offer of blindfolds and looked into the barrels of the guns as they shot us. When our bodies fell to the earth, they buried us beside the stockade.

The souls of my son and my brother-in-law went to be with our ancestors, but my spirit lingered in these mountains to watch over my people. I wanted to see if our sacrifice made any difference. If the white man would keep his word.

To my surprise, the white man ruled that the Quallatown Cherokee who lived outside the official boundaries of the Cherokee Nation were not required by law to emigrate, and that those Cherokee still hiding in the mountains might join with them and live freely.

We have grown in number through the years. Ten thousand Cherokee now reside in our ancient homeland. I guard their sleep and watch over their dreams as they live and work, laugh and love and die in these mountains, carrying on the traditions and wisdom passed to us from our ancestors.

The Cherokee's tale ceased abruptly as the good-natured shouts of children echoed along the path. From the sound of it, they were heading toward the bypass trail that led back to the parking lot. They raced past, followed rapidly by their puffing parents.

The sound snapped Joe out of his trance. He glanced toward the noisy day trippers and then turned back toward his storytelling companion. The stump was empty. Joe blinked and shook his head, trying to clear it. Where had the Cherokee man gone? There wasn't time for him to walk away, or any place he could have gone without Joe observing it.

Goose bumps traveled up Joe's arms and legs. He shivered, remember the man's words. "We fell dead . . ."

In his dream-like state, Joe hadn't taken particular notice of them. But they came back to him now. Had he been talking to a ghost? Joe gasped and sprang to his feet, agitated by the thought. The man had seemed so real.

Joe took a long drink from his water bottle. His hand was shaking so hard, he spilled more water onto his shirt. Maybe he had he fallen asleep and dreamed the whole episode? Joe's stomach churned. This was ridiculous. He didn't believe in ghosts. He rubbed a hand across his eyes and then secured his water bottle before starting back down the trail.

Before the first turn, Joe hesitated and glanced back toward the old stump. A Cherokee man in traditional garb sat there, gazing out over the mountains. He turned his head and met Joe's gaze. The spirit of Tsali raised a hand in greeting as the astonished hiker stared bug-eyed at him, mouth agape. And then he disappeared.

10

Ghost Marker

Me and a couple buddies always go camping in the Smokies the first week in April. My wife called it an extended boys' night out, and that was about right. We'd fish and hike the trails, tell ribald tales around the campfire, and count the stars until we fell asleep.

We were using the Cosby Campground as our basecamp this year. We set up our tents on adjacent sites and had a communal area under a massive tarp we attached to the trees. Everything was normal the first night, including the bear sighting and chasing squirrels away while we ate our dinner.

My best friend Bob suggested a long hike for Saturday and he plotted out our route on the map before we turned in. Bob's ancestors had settled this part of the Smoky Mountains and lived here for generations, until they were bought out by the national park. This weekend was a bit of a homecoming for Bob.

We were up with the birds on Saturday and had hiked miles from our basecamp by the time we broke for lunch. We sprawled around a small clearing near the mountaintop, admiring the view through gaps in the trees and comparing notes on the trail

so far. It was Bob who realized we were dining on the ruins of an old settler home. Something about the shape of the clearing and the bushes thereabouts tipped him off.

After lunch, we poked around the clearing for a while. I was examining the site of a small spring, wondering if the rotted boards in the area were the remains of a springhouse when I spotted a weathered sign propped against the base of a tree. It was about the size of a placemat and it had some strange symbols drawn on it. There was a circle on the top, with lines radiating away from it to smaller circles drawn beneath. It was really bizarre. I couldn't take my eyes off it.

I was going to show my buddies, but something stopped me. It felt almost as if someone clamped a hand over my mouth. I can't rightly explain what happened next. I am a law-abiding citizen as a rule, and I didn't believe in taking relicts from a national park. But between one moment and the next, that strange sign was tucked away in my backpack and I was hiking back up to the trail, urging my buddies to get a move on.

I kept glancing over my shoulder as we walked away, as if I was watching for someone to catch up with us. Which was ridiculous. I tried not to think about the weathered sign in my backpack. I knew the right thing to do was to turn around and put it back by the spring. But at that moment, nothing couldn't have forced me to give it up.

I was the last one in line, and I kept turning to make a remark to a hiking companion who wasn't there. It was strange. When Bob came back to walk with me, he remarked on my jitters. "What's with you, man?" he asked. "You act like you've seen a ghost. Did something spook you in that clearing?"

"No," I said, a bit too quickly to be believed.

Bob studied me a moment. "You know I'll get it out of you, one way or another," he said. "You've never been able to lie to me, not since we were kids."

"It's nothing," I snapped.

Bob shrugged and let me step in front of him when the trail narrowed. I was doubly annoyed now. At myself for taking the sign and at Bob for making me feel guilty about it. I was also mad at Bob for interrupting my conversation with. . . . My brain stuttered to a halt at that juncture. Wait a second! Who did I think I was talking to? I shivered and quickened my pace, wanting to get away from the haunted stretch of woods.

Our group was exhausted by the time we got back from our hike. We'd made a huge loop through the mountains and had gotten rained on by a passing cloudburst. It was a relief to slip into my tent and change into dry clothes. I set my backpack down with a heavy thump and thought about the weathered sign. Small circles radiating from a larger one. I wondered what it meant.

Bob got a fire going, and we all settled down to eat and drink beer while the sun set behind the mountains. The clouds from the clearing storm turned fiery colors and then deepened to blues and purples before blending in with the night sky. I took a deep breath and relaxed. As long as I didn't think about the sign, I was at peace.

I was feeling pleasantly blurry by the time I staggered to my tent to get some shut eye. When I crawled inside, my flashlight showed everything in disarray. The crumpled sleeping bag was shoved into the far corner, clothes were strewn everywhere, and the contents of the backpack lay in a heap on the floor. The

GHOST MARKER

weathered sign was propped in a place of prominence against the tent wall where anyone could see it. I cursed and shoved the sign and my belongings into the backpack, wondering which of my buddies was messing with me.

It was probably Gene that done it. The thought came to me out of the blue. I nodded. Yeah, it was probably Gene. I'd have to give him what for in the morning.

I was in a foul mood when I went to sleep and was still grumpy when I got up in the morning. I locked everything but my daypack into the car before we left on our hike. I didn't want anybody else messing with the weathered sign.

Bob tiptoed around me like I was an angry bear all morning. It was really annoying. And I kept looking over my shoulder for Gene, who hung back as if he didn't want the rest of us to see him. After the prank he pulled on me last night, I guess that made sense.

I was ready for this weekend to be done. I stomped my way through the hike and didn't laugh at any of the jokes my buddies made when we stopped to hydrate or admire the view. One of the guys started ribbing me for talking like an 1800s settler, which I didn't appreciate. First Gene, now everybody. Couldn't a feller take a walk without folks messing with his head?

Bob gave me a strange look when I said this aloud. We were nearly back at camp, and I was never so grateful to see my newfangled tent. My grumpy mood had infected everyone, and we broke down our gear in silence and packed up the cars. Bob was sharing my ride home, durn it. He'd probably ask me about that weathered sign. Pesky as a young 'un, that Bob.

No surprise, Gene packed himself into the back seat near the backpack that held the weathered sign while Bob claimed

the front. I stared for a moment at the strange gears around the wheel. These automobiles were some durn complicated machinery. Give me a horse any day. I finally figured out how to turn the key and started poking at the other gadgets, trying to get the durned thing a-going. Before I could set it to working, Bob shouted my name so loud it set my ears to burning.

"Get out of the car. I'm driving," Bob said. His face was so stern, I obeyed at once.

I tried to get out, but I was strapped in by some goldurned flexible tie. I tugged uselessly at it several times, but I couldn't figure it out. That crazy Gene was pullin' another trick on me. I kept expectin' him to laugh at my struggles, but Gene stayed silent in the back seat.

Bob pushed a button by my hip and finally I was free of the pesky strap. We traded places, Bob and me, and he set that fancy automobile in motion, as slick as ya please. When had Bob learned to drive one of them fancy pieces?

"Why don't you tell me what happened at the settler's clearing we found yesterday," Bob said.

"Nothing happened," I snapped. "Ask Gene if you don't believe me."

Bob glanced sideways at me. "Who is Gene?" he asked carefully.

"Who is Gene? Are ya kidding me? Gene's our buddy that's setting there in the back," I snapped. Why in tarnation was Bob being so ornery?

"No one named Gene came on our camping trip," Bob said. "And there's no one sitting in the back seat."

I glared at him and turned around to ask Gene to talk sense into him. The back seat was empty. My jaw dropped. There was nothing there but my backpack. And the weathered sign, which had mysteriously slipped out of the zippered backpack and was now propped on the seat. The small circles radiating out from the big circle at the center seemed to glow before my dazzled eyes.

"I think I need help, Bob," I stammered, realization dawning.

Bob found a place to pull off the road. He stopped the car and looked at me. Then he looked into the back seat and saw the weathered sign. His face went blank for a moment, and then he crossed himself. Bob's mama was a Catholic and she'd taken her family to Mass every week since they were babies. Bob was raising his family the same way. He fumbled in his pocket and came out with a rosary. Oh boy. This was serious.

"Where did that sign come from?" he asked.

"I found it in the settler's clearing," I said reluctantly. "I don't know what it is, and I don't know why I took it. One minute I was looking at it, the next minute it was in my backpack."

"And now you are acting like a settler from the 1800s and you are talking about an invisible someone named Gene as if he's a close friend of yours." Bob had a way with words, I had to hand it to him.

"That about sums it up," I said, thinking carefully before I spoke so I sounded like me and not a settler.

"Do you know what those symbols mean?" asked Bob.

I shook my head.

"My granddaddy showed me an old sign like that once," Bob said. "He said it was a ghost marker. It showed the place where ghosts resided, and warned that if you lingered there, a ghost might follow you home."

My whole body started to shake. My stomach churned, and I suddenly threw open the door and vomited on the side of the road. I swiped at my mouth with my sleeve and closed the door.

"You think a ghost made me take that sign so it could come home with me?" I asked.

"Looks like it," Bob said evenly, handing me a bottle of water to wash away the lingering taste of vomit. I rinsed my mouth, opened the door again and spat out the water. I gulped the rest of it down, suddenly thirsty.

"Gene," Bob said aloud once I closed the door again. "You can't go home with him. His missus would tan your hide. Worse, she'd make you wash every day. And twice on Sundays."

The whole atmosphere in the car turned cold as ice.

"You'll be much happier on the mountain," Bob said. "I think we should take you back."

The air swirled around us as if a mini tornado had formed inside the car.

"Tell him 'no,'" Bob said, handing me the rosary.

I cleared my throat a few times and then told Gene he had to go back to his cabin. My hair stood on end when I said it, but the atmosphere in the car lightened. Suddenly, my mind was clear for the first time since yesterday's lunch. I lurched back in the car seat and stared in revulsion at the weathered sign. "We've got to take that back right now, Bob."

Bob nodded and started the car. He turned around and drove to the camp site.

"I think you'd better stay here," he advised me. I nodded shakily and watched him depart for the trail with his daypack, some bottled water, and the weathered sign.

I found a good fishing spot to while away the time until Bob came back without the ghost marker.

"Back where it belongs," Bob said. We piled into the car and drove away as fast as we could without breaking any laws.

"Thanks, man," I said after we passed out of the national park and turned toward home.

"Anytime," Bob replied.

11

Half Shaved

PIGEON FORGE, TENNESSEE

There's a spooky story told around these parts about a man named Ted that decided to sell his fancy property and head out on the Oregon Trail. He owned a nice house and some land just outside town, and he sold it for a bushel of silver. Now Ted was a wise man and he didn't say much about his plans. He just quietly prepared for his journey. But the fellow who bought the property wasn't so discreet, and word got around about Ted's bushel of silver.

The day before his departure, Ted decided he wanted to spruce himself up before taking on the wider world. He asked a fellow he knew that was good at barbering to come by the house to shave off his wild whiskers and give him a haircut. The barber dropped by with his razor and a big bottle of whiskey so they could raise a toast to Ted's new adventure. They set Ted up on a stool near the cook stove in the kitchen and the man started shaving off Ted's bushy beard. The barber completely removed the hair from the right half of Ted's face before he casually asked if Ted was done packing.

"Everything I need is the wagon," Ted said glibly. "It's all done but the hitching up. I'll be off at first light tomorrow."

"That's real good," said the barber. And quick as a whistle, he cut Ted's throat with the razor, digging so deep that his head was nearly severed from his body. The barber left him to bleed out on the kitchen floor while he ran out to the wagon to steal the bushel of silver. It wasn't there. He opened every box and looked under every board. No silver. He searched the house and the barn. No money.

"Ted must have buried it," the barber raged. But there was no telling where. He didn't see any signs of digging in the immediate vicinity. Going back into the house, the barber removed his razor and the bottle of whiskey so no one would know he'd been there and went home.

When Ted's family came over at first light to bid him farewell, they found him dead in a puddle of blood with his face half shaved and his head half off. No one knew who killed him.

When the new owner moved in, it was quickly apparent that the house was haunted. Doors banged open and closed. Windows sprang open and slammed shut. Furniture moved itself. When a phantom came staggering through the main room with his head half off and a razor in his head, the new owner fled in a panic and sold the house the next day.

The same thing happened over and over again. Someone would buy the house at a discount and abandon it within a few days. The bravest family lasted a whole week before they ran screaming from the property and never returned.

By this time, the house was so run-down and neglected that the latest owner despaired of ever getting it off his hands. So when a poor couple came to town looking for work and asked if there was an empty house where they could camp for a few days, the owner told them: "I've got a haunted property just

HALF SHAVED

outside town that nobody wants. I'd like to get it off my hands, so I'm willing to make a deal with you. If you can live in that house for a whole year without running away, I'll give you the deed for free."

The poor couple agreed at once. After all, how bad could it be? They walked out to the property carrying their little baby and were astonished to find a dilapidated but fancy house with cracked glass windows and multiple rooms. There was a large spooky barn out back and plenty of land thereabouts.

"We'll live like rich folks," the man told his wife. "I can't believe the owner wants to give this place away for free."

The wife wasn't so enthused. "If folks don't reckon to live in a fancy place like this, it means the ghost must be a real terror."

But they had nowhere else to go, so the couple took their small bundle of belongings into the house and had a good look around. There were two bedrooms, a nice sitting room, and a large kitchen. The rooms were filled with dusty furniture. It was the biggest house the couple had ever set foot in, and it even had a staircase up to a big open attic.

There were cobwebs and dirt everywhere. The roof needed repairing and some of the windows were completely shattered, letting the weather in. But there wasn't anything here that couldn't be fixed with a little hard work and some ingenuity.

It was growing dark, so the wife put her baby to bed and then started up the cookstove to make supper while her husband went outside to chop wood and inspect the barn. The kitchen was getting dark, so the wife lit a lantern so she could see. She was scrubbing down the worktable when a sudden cold breeze swirled through the air, snuffing the lantern and making the cracked windows rattle in their panes. The door opened

with a bang, and a white figure staggered into the room. Its head lolled against its shoulder, silvery blood streaming from a gaping wound in its neck. One side of its face was covered with a bushy beard while the other side was shaved bare. It carried a razor in its hand that it swung wildly about, as if it was trying to defend itself.

The wife shrieked in terror and flung herself between the ghost and the door to the bedroom where her baby slept. "Lord have mercy," she cried, grabbing a dusty old broom from the corner and holding it up like a weapon. "Don't you kill my baby!"

To her astonishment, the phantom froze in place. Their eyes locked over the razor and the raised broom. Then the phantom dropped its hand and tucked the razor into its belt. The wife relaxed and lowered her broom, though she did not release it, just in case this was a ploy to get under her guard.

"You are the first person to speak to me since my death," the phantom said. As it spoke, the ghastly elements of its haunting slowly faded away, leaving the wife facing a sad-eyed ghost with a half-shaved face. "I need your help. I want justice. I want my murderer to stand trial for what he did to me."

The phantom told the wife the name of the man who nearly sliced off his head and asked her to go to the authorities and have him arrested. When he came to trial, a witness would show up to substantiate her claim. As a reward, he would give her his bushel of silver.

The wife felt sympathy for the sad-eyed man who had gone to eternity with a half-shaved face, so she agreed to do what the phantom asked. The next morning, she went to the authorities and told them she was living in Ted's old home and she had found out who murdered him. The barber was arrested and a trial was arranged for the next day.

Most everyone in town came to the trial, and when the judge asked what he was charged with, the barber said: "Murder."

"How do you plead? Guilty or not guilty?" asked the judge.

Before the barber could answer, the door to the courtroom banged open and the temperature of the room plummeted. A silvery figure stalked through the door, carrying a sharp razor in his hand. His face was half shaved and his partially severed head lolled gruesomely against his shoulder as silvery blood poured out in a gusher.

When the barber saw the ghost, his eyes rolled back in panic. He gasped for air, clutched at his arm, and fell over dead. The phantom stalked over to his murder and threw the glowing razor on his dead body. Then he looked over the gaping crowd and said: "Justice is served." Then he vanished with a thunderclap and a brilliant flash of light.

When the couple came home from the trial, they found a gentle-eyed man with a trim beard and just a bit of a glow about his figure waiting on their doorstep. He led them into the woods a-piece and asked them to move a massive rock that was lodged in the earth.

"That's too heavy," the wife said, "even if we both lift together."

"I will help you," said the phantom.

So the couple lifted the massive rock, and it shifted easily for them, just as the ghost promised. Underneath was a hole filled with a bushel full of silver.

"Ma'am, I thank you," said the phantom to the wife and slowly faded away.

12

The Thirteenth of December

LITTLE TENNESSEE RIVER
GREAT SMOKY MOUNTAINS NATIONAL PARK

A huge rainstorm rolled in the evening of December 13, 1874. Inside the little house near the ford, Uncle Howard shivered and edged his chair closer to the fire. "That rain sure is beatin' hard tonight," he remarked to his wife.

Auntie Howard looked up from the quilt she was sewing and nodded. "It's comin' down s'hard I'm a-feared the roof will fall down!"

"Not hardly," Uncle Howard protested. "We made the roof good and tight. Nothin' short of an act o' God would bring it down. There's more to fear from the river flooding. T'aint no one with sense who'd cross the ford tonight."

"Not everyone hearabouts has sense," said Auntie Howard dryly.

Uncle Howard grinned at her and turned his attention back to his wood carving.

About 8 o'clock in the evening, Uncle Howard started feeling peckish. He set aside his carving and went to the kitchen area to hunt up a piece of bread. He was right next to the window when he heard a piercing scream that set his pulses pounding.

"What was that?" he cried, hurrying to the door. He pressed his ear to the wood, but all he could hear was the rain pouring down and the wind howling and blowing.

"Is one of them painter cats a-huntin'?" Auntie Howard asked, her face creased with concern.

"Maybe. I can't hear nothin' now but the storm," said Uncle Howard, straightening up and carrying his snack over to his chair by the fire. "It did sound uncommonly human."

The storm had cleared by the time Uncle Howard got up to tend to his stock. His morning chores were interrupted when a couple of men came running up in a panic. They'd found a body down by the ford.

"Who is it?" Uncle Howard asked, following them back to the site.

"Hit's John McWade! Whoever done it nearly took 'is head off'n his neck," the men told him.

Even with the heavy rains of the night before, there was still so much blood that Uncle Howard felt his stomach heave. He ran back to the house and ordered his wife to stay inside. Then he rode with the men to fetch the authorities.

The neighborhood was a-buzz with gossip that afternoon. Every fact about John McWade was aired as folks tried to figure out who had done him in.

John McWade had moved into the area about two years ago, and he didn't talk much about his past or where he came from. He was a terrible farmer, but he never lacked for money. The romantically inclined thought he was a rich man who'd been crossed in love and come to the mountains to forget his sorrows. Other folks thought he was dodging a crime. Folks looked on him with distrust, but his mild manner and willingness to help his neighbors soon calmed everyone's fears.

"He was a right kind man and he didn't deserve this," Auntie Howard told her closest neighbor over a cup of tea. "And to think, my husband heard the scream over the storm! We thought it was one of them painter cats. But it must have been McWade."

The neighbor shared her own news. "I just spoke with Missus Barnes. She lives next door to the McWade place, you know, and she said a stranger stopped by last night and asked for supper and some feed for his horse. While he was at the Barnes place, he asked a fair number of questions about McWade. The stranger departed right after supper, but with the dark and the rain and the terrible condition of the road, they reckon he wouldn't have reached the ford before 8 o'clock."

"That's the time my husband heard the scream," Auntie Howard breathed.

The two women clucked over their tea. This was highly suspicious.

"Did the Barnes talk to the officers about it?" asked Auntie Howard.

"Mister Barnes went down to talk to them as soon as he heard about the murder," the neighbor confirmed. "They were on their way to McWade's house to try to find somethin' that would tell them who done it."

"Well it sure enough wasn't a thief that done him in," said Auntie Howard. "My husband told me they found $100 on him and a gold watch. A thief wouldn't have left 'em behind."

The murder was the talk of the community for several weeks. But no one was arrested, and the rumors slowly died away. It was an unsolved mystery, one of many floating around these hills. McWade was well on his way to being forgotten.

When December 13 rolled around again, it was as different as a night could be. The sky was clear, the moon was shining, and the frost was creeping across the ground as the clock ticked around to 8 o'clock.

Uncle Howard was setting with his wife by the fire, as before, when he heard a faint scream down by the ford. It sounded like someone calling for help. He and Auntie Howard looked at one another in alarm as the cry came again, louder this time. The screams increased in strength as Uncle Howard leapt up from his chair, but they ceased before he was halfway across the room. Then the latch on the door started to rattle, followed by a rapping on the window. Uncle Howard gazed through the pane into the face of the murdered John McWade. His eyes were wild with fear, his face twisted in a rictus of pain, and blood was pouring from a long gash across his throat. The air in the cabin grew icy cold as the Howards gazed with horror upon the phantom. Then it was gone.

Auntie Howard wrung her hands and began weeping hysterically. Uncle Howard wasn't sure if he should comfort her or join her. His nerves were a wreck.

The story was the talk of the neighborhood for a week or more. Half the folks believed it utterly and half thought Uncle Howard was ailing and needed to see a doctor. But everyone agreed it made a spooky tale to tell around the fire when the young 'uns wanted to hear about ha'nts.

Most folks had plumb forgotten about the ghost by the time December 13 rolled around again. Kabel Gordon certainly didn't have the story in mind when he approached the ford in

THE THIRTEENTH OF DECEMBER

his wagon around 8 o'clock. He'd crossed the river hundreds of times in clear and stormy weather and never had a problem. But that night, his team shied and balked in turns, refusing to go near the water. All of sudden, a white figure rose from the side of the road in the very place where the body was found. As it grew solid, it morphed into the figure of McWade.

The horses bolted in terror, pulling the wagon through the ford at a dead run. As they reached the solid ground on the far side, an appalling scream ripped through the night air, making Gordon's hair stand on end. All the fear and pain and anger in the world was caught up in that scream. Gordon realized he was reliving McWade's death. Uncle Howard had been right about the ghost.

Uncle Howard's triumph was short-lived, for he passed away in the spring, and his wife went to live with her married son. The house by the ford was sold to a man named Daniels who came from Virginia. He moved in with his wife and three children just before summer, and they were well settled in by December 13.

That night, a storm thundered into the area with the same force as the gale on the night of the murder. The wind howled and roared, rain poured out of the sky, and at 8 o'clock precisely, the Daniels family heard someone screaming for help down by the ford. The sound grew louder and closer. Daniels and his eldest son made a grab for their guns. Suddenly the screams ceased. Before they could open the door, the latch rattled and someone tapped at the window. The family looked out the rain-streaked pane into the ghastly face and panic-stricken eyes of a man. His hair was disheveled, and he had a horrible gash cut into his throat. Blood gushed from the wound, staining his coat and shirt. The specter gazed pleading at the Daniels family and then vanished without a trace, leaving the household in an uproar.

A frightened Daniels went the next morning to the neighbor's house to relate the strange haunting of the previous night. He described the man so accurately that his neighbor knew he had seen McWade's ghost. The neighbor told him about the murder and the ghost it had spawned. Horrified, Daniels went right out and rented another house a mile down the river and moved his family into it before nightfall.

And so the old Howard place lay abandoned. Such was its reputation that no one in the neighborhood would go into it. Even the animals avoided the property.

Now it happened one year that a party of young men from the east came into the neighborhood to hunt.

When they heard about the haunted house, they were eager to see the ghost. Five of them repaired to the vicinity of the house on the evening of December 13 and they waited in the darkness for 8 o'clock to arrive. Two lost their nerve and fled the house before the appointed hour. The others waited in suspense, checking the clock by the light of a match every few moments.

The men were crouched in the bushes midway between house and ford, hoping to catch sight of the ghost wherever it appeared. Three minutes before 8 o'clock, a white figure rose out of the ground near the ford and solidified into the form of a young man. He floated toward the river and stopped a few feet from the water's edge. Suddenly, the spirit cringed back and began struggling with an unseen assailant. Then it screamed in terror and a bloody gash appeared across its throat. The ghost writhed as if in great pain, staggered a few steps and tumbled to a heap on the ground. A moment later, a cloudy specter rose from the heap in a shower of sparks, and raced screaming toward the abandoned Howard house.

"That must have been his final thought, the night of the murder. He wished to summon help before it was too late and now his ghost keeps trying to save him," an awestruck spectator murmured. "I wonder if he realizes he is dead?"

"I don't know, and I don't care," said one of his companions. "I've had enough of ghosts to last me a lifetime! Let's get out of here."

The men beat a hasty retreat, vowing to leave the ghost hunting to others in the future.

Folks living in the area say that McWade's ghost still enacts his final moments at the ford. Anyone crossing it at 8 o'clock on December 13 can still see the phantom, if they dare.

PART TWO
Powers of Darkness and Light

13

The Mule-Eared Chair

GATLINBURG, TENNESSEE

I could not believe my eyes when I saw the price on the antique mule-eared chair in the small shop in Gatlinburg. No way was this a real settler's chair. Not at that price. I got down on my knees and studied the chair from every angle. It seemed authentic. Shaved rear posts, curved slightly inward. Slat-backed seat. Very sturdy. It looked like the support posts were made out of maple and these rounded struts were probably hickory. And the patterns on the chair back and legs were unique. I blinked a few times, startled. It looked like an Odom chair out of Shell Creek, probably made in the early 1800s. If that was the case, this was a real steal. I noticed that one of the legs wasn't a perfect match for the others. It must have been replaced at some point, I decided.

I purchased the chair and set it carefully in the back of the truck. It would hold a place of honor on my back porch. I couldn't wait to show my husband! We lived in a modernized cabin just outside Gatlinburg, in the foothills of the Smoky Mountains, where we both grew up. I knew he would love this piece of our state's history.

We brought dessert out to the back porch that night and sat watching the night settle in. The mule-eared chair was quite comfortable. I was happily surprised. I settled back and sipped my tea while my husband ate apple pie and chatted about his day.

The first stars were coming out when I felt a bit of a twinge in my nerves. The chair didn't feel as comfortable as it had when I first sat down. I wanted to shift my position to relieve the tension in my back and legs, but I was feeling lethargic. The idea of moving a single muscle did not appeal.

I laid my head against the back of the chair and closed my eyes. I was drifting in and out of consciousness when the dream started. I was leaning into the fireplace to stir a boiling cauldron of some nasty-smelling liquid. When I straightened, I saw a one-room cabin with herbs hanging from the ceiling, a small bed in the corner and a table with half-finished salves and potions on it. My eyes passed over each item, and I knew exactly what they did. The blue jar was for aches and pains. The salves would help itchy feet. The brown bottle was a love philter. And powdered herbs helped with snakebite.

I felt a jabbing pain in my arm and jerked awake. My husband leaned over me with a concerned look on his face. "You'll hurt your neck if you keep sleeping like that," he said, pulling me out of the mule-eared chair. "Come on, it's almost time for our show."

Our show? Oh right. We were watching season two of something-or-other. My mind was still dazed by the dream. It seemed so real.

About halfway through the episode, I had to run to the kitchen for antiseptic. I had a scratch on my right arm. I had no idea how it got there, but it ached something awful.

I dragged around the house the next day. I worked out of a home office and I was generally very productive. But I couldn't keep my mind on any of my projects. I thought fresh air would help, so took a folding tray table outside and set it in front of my antique chair. It was the perfect height for my laptop. Breathing deeply of the fresh air, I started typing.

I don't know when I fell asleep. One moment, I was emailing a client. The next I was walking down a dirt path toward the one-room cabin, muttering curses to myself over some settler who had disrespected me. I'd show him. I was more than a simple herbalist. I knew the dark secrets too. If he weren't careful, none of his livestock would survive.

My head hit the keyboard and I jerked awake, barely in time to catch the tottering tray table and save my laptop from a damaging fall. What the heck? I never fell asleep during the day. Both my arms were aching, and my body felt glued to the chair. I was too heavy to lift myself up.

That was nonsense! I gave myself a pep talk and forced myself out of the chair. I needed a drink of water and another bandage. There was a red scratch on my left arm, identical to the one I'd treated last night.

My husband got home around six. He took one look at my tired face and ordered a pizza. Then he sent me to bed early. Rest sounded good. I must be coming down with something, I decided. But I had no fever, no cough, no stomach symptoms. Just a dragging tiredness.

I felt better in the morning. No weird dreams disturbed my sleep and I'd regained some of my energy. The cuts on my arms still stung when I treated them with antiseptic, but I thought they looked a bit better.

I had to work quickly to make up for my unproductive day. By early afternoon, I was caught up, so I rewarded myself with a cup of coffee and a pastry on the back porch. The mule-eared chair was so comfortable. I hunkered down happily, letting go of my worries. This was the life!

As before, the longer I sat, the achier I felt. But I was tired. Too tired to shift my body. Too tired to keep my eyes opened. . . .

There was a steady stream of valley folks coming to the door, wanting potions to stop the fever that gripped the residents of the small community. It was good for my business. And best of all, no one suspected I was the true cause of the illness. I'd set a little curse in the center of the small village, and it was slowly radiating out to each home. Anyone who was on the cusp got sick. Anyone who was already ill got sicker. And I got rich healing them up. I gloated over the cauldron which held both curse and cure, depending on how large a dose you took. That disrespectful fool would get a very large dose and see how he liked it.

The pain in my arms was so sharp it ripped me out of my sleep. I'd spilled my cold coffee down my shirt, and my wrists were bleeding as if I'd slashed them. I shouted and ran for the door, forgetting the china plate in my lap. It shattered against the floor of the porch, pastry crumbs scattering everywhere.

I dabbed at the open cuts on my wrist. How did I get them? What in the world was going on? I added two more bandages to my collection and changed into a dry shirt. Then I went outside to clean up the mess. I studied the mule-eared chair from a safe distance. My tiredness, the cuts, the dreams. They all started when I brought the darned chair home.

My husband found me brooding on the porch, staring at the mule-eared chair from the opposite end with an outdoor pillow clutched in front of me like a shield. He did a double take when he saw all my bandages and the grim look in my eyes.

"What in the world?" he asked.

"That chair is haunted," I said.

"Wait. What?" he asked.

"It's giving me dreams. And I think it's the source of my scratches."

My husband examined the chair. "Not possible. The wood is perfect—no splinters. And how can a chair give you dreams?"

"I don't know. But it does. You sit in it and see what happens," I said briskly.

He sat down, waited for a moment, then spread his arms expressively. "No scratches. No dreams."

"Wait a few minutes. It's just getting warmed up," I said. "I'll bring dinner out here. You stay put."

I dished up spaghetti and meatballs, tossed a salad, and served my husband on the same tray table I'd nearly destroyed with my head. I brought a second serving for myself and sat far away in the wicker chair, watching my husband.

"I love you, honey, but I think you are crazy," he said between mouthfuls. "This chair is so comfortable, I could sit here all night."

When we finished eating, I made coffee and we sat watching the stars come out. When I looked over, I saw my husband dozing in the mule-eared chair. I waited. Nothing happened. I waited some more. He started snoring. Finally, I got up and shook his shoulder. He came awake and looked at me blearily. "Are you did dreaming? Did you see the witch?"

He blinked and rubbed his eyes. "Dang it, this chair is too comfy for my own good. I almost did spend the night out here."

"Did you see the witch?" I asked impatiently.

THE MULE-EARED CHAIR

He yawned and sort of rolled out of the chair. He looked exhausted. "I dunno. I can't remember if I was dreaming. Want to watch more of our show tonight? Or maybe not. I'm beat. Let's wait til tomorrow."

He scooped up the tray table and started for the back door. I caught a glimpse of his right arm in the light streaming from the kitchen window and gasped. "Look at your arm!"

"What about my arm?" he raised it, trying to see in twilight. There was a scratch on his arm in the identical place where my first scratch had appeared.

Chills ran up and down my spine. I was hoping I'd imagined the whole thing. But this was proof! There was something wrong with the chair.

My husband looked stunned. "How did that get there?" He stared at me, his eyes going so wide I saw the whites. He turned back to stare at the chair. "Good Lord Almighty," he whispered.

"I'm getting rid of it tomorrow," I said. "The antiques shop will buy it back. Or I'll give it to a thrift shop. It is not staying here!"

My husband nodded and went inside to treat his cut. I cleaned up the dinner things and went into the house, giving the chair a wide berth.

After breakfast, I backed up the truck to the edge of the porch and went to pick up the chair. As soon as my hands closed around the wood, I was overwhelmed with fatigue. I fought it, lifting the chair and taking one step, then two. It felt like I was walking through deep mud. Third step. Fourth step.

I sank to the porch floor with the chair in my arms. And saw a torch-bearing mob stalking up the path to my one-room cabin. They were shouting and chanting my name. I had to run!

I had to hide. But those clever cowards had sent men around the back. They cornered me, and the disrespectful fellow accused me of killing his daughter. He grabbed my chair—my prized possession—and snapped off a leg, then he strode toward me with the sharp jagged part held in front of him like a spear.

"Wake up," my husband shouted, shaking my shoulders. He sounded hysterical. "Please wake up!"

The chair lay on the floor next to me, and my husband splashed a full glass of water over my face. It wasn't the first one. My clothes were soaked.

"Oh thank God," he groaned when I opened my eyes, and clutched me to his chest. I think he actually cried in relief.

"What are you doing here? I thought you left for work," I gasped into his shirt.

"I left my ID in the kitchen and came back for it. I saw you lying there with the chair in your arms. I thought you were dead," he said gruffly.

He picked me up as if I was still his teenage girlfriend and carried me to our bedroom. "You are going to rest. And I am going to take that blasted chair to the thrift shop. No arguing. I'll be back to check on you."

I nodded. That was fine by me. That final dream had scared the wits out of me. I needed space to rest and reflect.

I dozed off at once and didn't wake until evening. My husband had dinner for me on a tray, and he also had news. "I found out about the chair," he said, sitting beside me on the bed and stealing French fries from my plate. "I spoke to the local historian and he'd heard about it. It is called the vampire chair, because the woman who owned it was found buried face down in the center of a mountain road with the leg of an Odom mule-eared chair impaled in her chest. The folks that found her figured she must have been a vampire of some kind, or maybe a witch. No one knows for sure. The chair you bought came from her cabin. They believe it was the leg from the vampire chair that was used to kill her."

My body went cold. I drew a shaky breath. That tallied with my last dream. And I'd noticed the mismatched leg the day I bought the chair.

"Anyway, folks all through this part of Tennessee have had bad encounters with the vampire chair. It's been just about everywhere and the effects on each owner are similar to the ones we experienced. It lures you in, makes you feel comfortable, and then leeches your strength. Sometimes people are cut up like we were. Some folks have dreams. Lucky us, we got the full suite of symptoms."

"Hurray," I said sarcastically. "Did the historian say anything about after-effects? Will the evil spirit linger here or did we banish it when we got rid of the chair?

"It should be gone for good," my husband said cheerfully. "But just in case, I called the pastor and asked him to come over and do a house blessing for us."

Relief washed through me. "Great idea. You've got brains, brawn, *and* beauty! What a guy."

"That's why you married me," he said smugly, and went to the kitchen to get us both some dessert.

14

The Nunnehi

FRANKLIN, NORTH CAROLINA

My parents died of the fever when I was a baby, so I was raised by my grandmother, who often told me stories of the Nunnehi, the Immortals. They are spirit folk who live in the high places of the land, and they are invisible to us mortals.

Grandmother described the wonderful dwellings they built for themselves in the heights, at the bare tops of the tallest mountains. When the sun shone brightly, I would gaze upward, straining my eyes in an attempt to catch a glimpse of those wondrous buildings. But I could not make them out. Once after a thunderstorm, as the dark clouds broke into tiny pieces around the mountain peaks, I thought I glimpsed a golden rooftop shining in a beam of sunlight between two clouds. But I blinked and it was gone.

"Why are the Nunnehi invisible?" I asked, leaning on Grandmother's knee as she stirred a pot full of delicious-smelling broth.

"They aren't always invisible," my grandmother said. "They show themselves to mortals sometimes. Let me tell you a story about the Nunnehi." She gave me a bowl of broth, and I sipped the warm liquid as I listened.

"A Nunnehi man appeared to my father once," Grandmother began. "My father had fallen from an isolated ridge while hunting. Father feared for his life. He was far from the normal hunting grounds, and he could not walk with a broken leg. Suddenly a tall man with eyes that glinted gold appeared and knelt beside my father. The man was an Immortal, come from the heights to help him. The Nunnehi tended the leg and then lifted my father as if he weighed no more than a baby. He carried my father back to the village, eight miles away, entered his lodge, and set him down on the bed. Then the Immortal vanished."

I gazed wide-eyed at Grandmother. How lucky Great-Grandfather had been, to be saved by an Immortal. I longed to see a Nunnehi. But it was very rare to meet one. Only one or two had been glimpsed since my great-grandfather's time.

I grew quickly, as all girls do, and found I had a great skill with herbs and medicines. The village medicine man sent me to apprentice with my cousin, who was a wise woman and healer living in the next village and my grandmother came to live with us.

The healing work was absorbing. I was so taken up in my studies that I had neither the time nor patience to be courted by any of the young warriors-in-training at home or in the wise woman's village. As the other girls sought for husbands, I sought roots and herbs and made poultices and teas. My grandmother frequently lamented over my single state. She would list off all the promising young warriors in the surrounding villages while I stirred the cook pot and mended my clothes, often torn by brambles as I rambled over the mountains searching for rare herbs. Grandmother had her heart set on me making a match during the upcoming harvest festival, when people from all the villages would gather and dance. She started making jewelry and decorating a new outfit for me to wear to the festival while I steeped medicines and learned healing lore from my teacher.

A month before the anticipated harvest dance, I left the lodge before dawn, determined to find wild ginseng for my wise woman, whose supply was running low. It was a frustrating day, filled with every variety of herb I could want, except ginseng. I went farther and farther afield, barely noticing the growing clouds, the hushed landscape. When the sun abruptly disappeared, I looked up and saw a dense mist pouring into the woods. I tried to outpace it, which was my undoing. One unseen root was all it took to trip up my speeding feet, and I tumble off the path and down several feet before a tree stopped my fall. As soon as I attempted to rise, I knew I was in trouble. My ankle hurt so bad I expelled my breakfast. My gathering basket with its healing herbs lay tumbled a few yards away, out of reach for now. And the fog continued its decent, enveloping me and obscuring woods, ridge, and the trail above. I uttered a curse that would have shocked my grandmother and then shuffled carefully—and painfully—around until my back was to the tree. I would have to wait until the mist cleared to treat and bind up my ankle. And I would need a crutch of some sort to help me get home.

I sat and shivered as cold drops of water formed on my skin. I desperately wanted a fire, but my flint was in the gathering basket and it would be too dangerous (and painful) to search for firewood. I drummed my fingers on my thighs, watching impatiently as the mist grew thicker. Grandmother and the wise woman would worry if I did not come home tonight.

I wakened from a painful doze when I heard a man's voice singing cheerfully in the mist. I'd never heard the tune before, or the clever words both praising and teasing the mist that obscured the whole mountain. I listened with a smile, and then realized that this man might help me, if he knew I was in need. But I was yards below the trail and he would pass me by in the fog. I called out to the man, and the singing stopped.

"Where are you?" he asked from somewhere above me, and I did my best to describe my location.

A moment later, a man appeared, swinging himself easily down the steep slope as if it were broad daylight. He was finely dressed, with a hunter's weapons and a pack strapped on his back. His face was clever and striking rather than handsome. When our gazes met, golden eyes twinkled at me in the gloomy shadows. They were unlike anything I'd seen before. I knew at once that he was a Nunnehi. He had to be. Who else could walk so freely in a blinding fog? I gaped at him like a stunned child. I had not expected my family history to repeat itself. But here was another Immortal coming to the aid of someone who stumbled off the path.

The Nunnehi said something to me, but I didn't make out his words through the buzzing in my brain. His grin widened at my astonished expression and he repeated: "May I look at your ankle?"

This time, his words penetrated. I nodded and added a breathless affirmative.

The Nunnehi's examination was brief but painful. The pain snapped me out of my shock, and as I gritted my teeth to bear it, I noted that the man's technique was as expert as that of my wise woman. He was obviously a skilled healer.

"The ankle is not broken," he said.

"No," I said. "I did not think so. But I have lost my herbs and I have nothing to bind it."

He blinked and sat back on his heels. "You are a healer?" he asked sharply.

"A healer in training. I was trying to refresh my supply of ginseng when the fog rolled in. And I was fool enough to try to outrun it, with disastrous results, as you have observed."

"We all make mistakes from time to time," he said.

"Mine tend to be few," I said, "but when I make one, it is either humiliating or disastrous. And on one special occasion, it was both!"

He laughed. "I think I want to hear that story," he said, removing a piece of hide from his hunting bag and cutting small binding strips from it.

"I think I want to conceal that story," I retorted.

But he wheedled it out of me, to help take my mind off the next painful moments as he plastered my ankle with herbs and bound it up. He did it better than I could. Better even than my wise woman.

"Come, I will take you home," he said when he was done. "Where do you live?"

I told him the name of the village where I lived with my teacher.

"I know it," the Immortal man said and swung me up into his arms as if I was a child.

"I can walk," I protested, though we both knew it was a lie.

He chuckled deeply, sending a small shiver of delight down my spine. Then he told me a story of one of his funnier mistakes, and I laughed so hard I was afraid he would drop me.

We swapped amusing anecdotes in the fog, which the Nunnehi navigated as easily as broad daylight. Far too soon, we came to the outskirts of the village, only steps away from my lodge.

"Here we are," the man said, setting me down at the foot of a large tree. "Hold still a moment."

He stepped to the nearest tree and snapped off a sturdy branch with an inhuman strength that took my breath away. Using his knife, he quickly stripped it of bark and fashioned a rough crutch.

He frowned. "Not my best work," he said, "but it will do for now."

He helped me to my feet and made sure the crutch was the right size.

"And what will you give me for my aching sides?" I asked with a smile. "For you have given me a stitch with all your tales."

He laughed. "I believe my stitch is quite as large as yours, Healer. Fare you well." He vanished, and the fog swirled uncertainly around the place where he stood before filling in the gap.

I did not move for a long time. Once again, my mind was a roaring, fizzing blank. Finally a thought surfaced from the dazzling mess. *Foolish girl. You've fallen in love with an Immortal.*

After they finished fussing over my injury, Grandmother and the wise woman scolded me for traveling alone in such dangerous fog. They said nothing about the lost gathering basket, which was kind, but I knew I would spend hours making another to replace it. I didn't tell them about meeting the Nunnehi man. It would needlessly worry them, for I did not think we would ever meet again. But I hugged the precious memory to my heart, wishing I had remembered to ask his name.

THE NUNNEHI

In the morning, I found my gathering basket filled with ginseng at the entrance to my lodge. A beautifully carved crutch leaned against the wall beside it. I picked up the crutch with trembling fingers and studied it. Blooming herbs were carved around the shaft with little birds peaking through the leaves. The cross-piece on top was a carved bear rolling humorously in a stream. The wise woman, exiting the lodge behind me, exclaimed over the gifts and then eyed me crossly. "What haven't you told me about yesterday?" she asked tartly. And the whole story came out.

The wise woman didn't speak for many minutes when I finished. She gazed thoughtfully into the cook fire and then nodded. "Thank you for telling me," she said. "I do not believe we should discuss this with your grandmother. She would worry." I nodded in agreement.

She made no further comment, which surprised me. I had expected stern warning and cautions, at the very least. But she said nothing about the state of my heart, for which I was grateful. And she set me a series of tasks that kept me so busy for the next few weeks that I had little time to dream of clever Nunnehi men.

I threw myself into all my normal activities, hoping they would help me forget. Wishful thinking. Each time I reached for my crutch or used ginseng in a medicine, I found myself remembering the laughing Nunnehi. At those moments I would abruptly stop whatever I was doing and stare blankly into space until the memory faded. Often a funny tale he told me during our walk down the mountain would spring to my mind and I'd laugh aloud for no apparent reason. I know it worried the wise woman, and my grandmother.

I hardly noticed when harvest time came. The festival on which Grandmother had pinned her hopes had no attraction for me now. But Grandmother was determined I should go. She thought a husband would snap me out of this strange inattentiveness.

In the end, I went to the dance to please her. People came from all over the settlement to celebrate the harvest in our village. There were men everywhere: tall ones, small ones, ugly ones, handsome ones. I hardly noticed. I sat beside the wise woman, using my weak ankle as an excuse to skip the activities. Grandmother, sitting nearby with my aunt and uncle, watched me sharply. I could tell she wanted me to dance. But I couldn't.

I turned away from the laughing crowd—and came face-to-face with a golden-eyed man with a merry smile. I gaped at him, my eyes bulging in shock. "How is your ankle?" he asked, taking my hand and leading me to a seat near one of the fires.

I spent the rest of the night talking with the Immortal, swapping stories as we had before and laughing so much that everyone around us laughed too. He was just the same as I remembered, clever and striking rather than handsome. And he had a basket full of carvings that he passed out to the children.

Grandmother watched us triumphantly. She knew a man would snap me out of my lethargy. But the wise woman looked worried. And I didn't blame her. A small piece of my heart ached, for this magical evening would not last. And then he would be gone forever.

Too soon, the festival ended and the people departed for their villages, calling out their farewells and promises to meet again. My smiling friend left with the final group, pressing a small gift into my hand before he departed. I watched him go, pain searing my chest. At least now I had a name to cherish. "Goodbye, Laughing Bear." I whispered.

I felt the wise woman's presence beside me and straightened slowly, like an old woman, to look into her kind eyes. "It is time to go," she said, and led me home as if I were an injured child. When I was alone, I took out the small gift the Nunnehi had pressed into my hand. It was the carving of a bear rubbing his back against a tree. The humorous look on the scratching bear's face pulled a watery chuckle from me.

Winter howled into the village within days of the harvest festival. An early blizzard snowed us in, rapidly followed by another. Time blurred as days became weeks. There was little time for the warriors to hunt, and the harvesting had been cut short by the blizzards. The villagers rationed their food, and the wise woman and I were kept busy dealing with frost-bit fingers and winter colds.

Many villagers commented on my quiet demeanor. "You have lost your smile," one old auntie said. I smiled to please her, but she shook her head. "Something is missing," she said, and patted my cheek in sympathy.

"Nothing is amiss, Auntie," I said. Just my heart.

At the height of a mid-winter storm, I was awakened by a soft thud on the wall of the lodge. Did someone need help? I looked across the banked fire toward the wise woman, who was fast asleep. Then I pulled a blanket around me and went to investigate in case someone needed our services. On the threshold, I found a bear carving the size of my fist. It was warm as summer with no snowflakes on it, although snow hurtled down from the sky. The small bear's head was tilted back as if it were laughing. It made me chuckle.

I gazed out into the snow-swirled darkness. The storm was so thick I could not see to the next lodge. There were no footprints leading toward or away from our home. "Thank you," I whispered into the storm, fighting back tears. I hid the bear carving under my sleeping blanket and wept until morning.

Our medicinal supplies were all but gone by the time the spring sun warmed enough to melt some of the deep snow. It was too early for any herbs to grow, but the wise woman sent me to find medicinal roots, sap and branches to boost our meager stores. I set out with my gathering basket, wrapped up tight against the cold. I used my former crutch as a walking stick. It was a lovely day, with just a hint of spring about it. The snow was slippery from the melt-off, and the fresh air smelled lovely after the wood smoke and body odors of too many days spent inside the village homes. My heart felt lighter outside. The Nunnehi might have put a dent in it, but there were still lovely sights to enjoy and worthwhile work to do. I would never marry, I decided, but I could enjoy the life I had.

I came at last to the riverbank, where the waters had already begun to swell with the snow melt. Sitting on an old stump on the far side of the water was the clever and striking Nunnehi. He was putting the finishing touches on a large carving. Wood chips were scattered around him in the snow. He wore no blanket for warmth. Indeed, the snow around him was melting faster than could rightly be accounted for, since he sat in the shade.

I used my former crutch to pull some evergreen branches close to me and clipped off needles to put into my basket.

"It is a fine day, is it not, Healer?" the Nunnehi asked.

"A fine winter day, yes," I replied, searching the tree trunk for resin. "But I am eager for spring. Our supplies are running low."

"The last winter storm has passed," the Nunnehi said, inspecting the carving in his hands. "Spring is well on its way. Look at your feet."

I peered down and saw tiny white flowers peeping up at me through the melting snow. My eyes widened. I knew they had not been there when I approached the tree.

"Are you helping things along?" I accused, shifting my attention back to the Nunnehi. I jumped in surprise, for he was suddenly standing beside me. How he had crossed the swollen river I did not know. His golden eyes studied me intently.

"You are too thin," he said. "And your eyes are sad. For whom do you weep?"

I turned my head away, unwilling to speak of such matters. The movement dislodged something from my gathering basket. He stooped and picked it up, a smile lighting his face. It was the laughing bear carving left on my threshold during the storm.

"So what do you think of him?" he asked, gesturing at the funny bear in his hand, and then to the swimming bear on the cane and the scratching bear just visible through the fir twigs in the basket.

"He is a bit of a trickster," I replied. "But I like his stories."

"A trickster? Not he," the Nunnehi said. "A rascal maybe. And a healer. He leaves the trickstering to Coyote and Crow." He touched the gathering basket, and it was filled at once with herbs, roots, branches, and twigs. Everything we needed for our supplies.

"Would you join your life with a rascal, Healer?" he asked.

I flushed crimson, then looked him in the eye and nodded shyly. "But I will not leave my grandmother," I said. "She is old and depends upon me."

"I would not ask you to," Laughing Bear said. "She will come and live with us and will help take care of our many children." He grinned at me. I blushed at the thought of many children and playfully tapped his nose.

Taking my hand, he led me back to the lodge. My grandmother and the wise woman were waiting outside the door. The wise woman had packed my things into a basket. Beside her, my grandmother held her own basket along with a carefully wrapped bundle of wedding clothes she had made for me. She had been working in secret on the beautiful garments ever since the harvest dance.

My eyes widened. "How did they know I was leaving?" I asked my Nunnehi suitor.

"I may have stopped by to ask your grandmother for your hand in marriage," Laughing Bear said with a sly grin.

I shook my carved crutch at him and he chuckled.

"Here are your things," the wise woman said, handing them to me with a smile. The Nunnehi presented her with his new carving: A laughing bear and his lady.

And so I married my Immortal, and he took me and my grandmother to live with him in the golden-roofed city on the mountaintop.

15

The Cat's Paw

OCONALUFTEE RIVER VALLEY
GREAT SMOKY MOUNTAINS NATIONAL PARK

It just so happened that Jack was down on his luck. He'd run out of money and so he took to wandering about, looking for work. That's how he found himself in this here valley. Now one little village hereabouts had never prospered from the time it was first settled. It was rumored that a secret coven of witches lived nearby and made life a misery for anyone that crossed them. Cows went dry. Pigs dropped dead in their pens. Chickens wouldn't lay. Things round here were a right mess.

Now Jack heard tell of a mill owner who was having more trouble than most. His new mill was said to be cursed and nobody would hire on with him. The owner was willing to pay top dollar to anyone brave enough to take on his cursed mill. So Jack headed to the owner's house and said to him: "I hear you need some help."

"Yessir, I do," the miller said. "I've got me a new mill, but its cursed. Every durned feller I've hired to run it was killed on his first night. Something poisoned 'em. If I can't lift the curse on the place, I'll lose all my money."

"I ain't skeered of no curse," Jack boasted. "Take me down there and I'll run your mill for you."

The two men walked down to the site of the new mill and looked the place over. The mill was done up real nice and the equipment was in good order. The owner had even fixed up an old log house with a fireplace, so the miller had a place to eat and sleep. The only strange thing about the log cabin was twelve little windows high up on the walls that didn't bring in much light.

"I'll take the job," Jack said. "And I won't get poisoned tonight neither."

"Suit yourself. It's your funeral," the owner of the mill said. "I'll give you half the wages up front, and some rations for your supper tonight. You can start right away."

Word spread like wildfire through the cove. Folks were so glad the new mill was running that they lined up to get their corn ground. Jack was kept busy from sunup to sundown. He was plumb tuckered by the time the last person paid for their grinding and headed home.

Jack had just shut down the equipment and turned the water out of the mill race when along came a one-eyed feller with a long gray beard, riding an ornery mule. Jack sighed when he saw the sack of corn on the feller's back, but he walked over to greet 'im.

"How-do, Jack," the old feller said.

Jack was surprised. "How'd you know my name?" he asked. "I ain't never seen you before."

"I'm a stranger to you," said the old feller. "But I know many things, Jack. Now I've come a long way and I wonder if'n you could grind some corn for me. I know it's passed quittin' time, but I couldn't get here sooner."

"Sure, I'll help you out," Jack said. "Wait here for a-piece while I get the mill started and then I'll do you right."

Jack turned on the waterwheel and ground up the man's corn for him. When he carried the heavy sack of meal back to the mule, the old feller said: "Jack, you is the first one that done right by me at this new mill. I've got a reward fer ya."

"T'aint necessary, sir," Jack said politely. "Hit was my pleasure."

But the old feller insisted. He pulled a silver knife out of his ragged coat pocket and handed it to Jack. "Hit's good against witches," he told Jack.

The knife was a real work of art. Jack admired it and thanked the old feller. Then he helped settle the sack of corn meal on the mule and watched him ride away into the dark.

Jack put the silver knife into his pocket and walked to the log cabin to build up a fire and fix him some supper. The moon was rising, and it shone in the twelve small windows, making the inside of that log cabin bright as day.

Jack was cutting up his ration of meat with the silver knife when suddenly the whole room went dark. If it weren't for the fire in the hearth, Jack couldn't have seen anything at all. He looked up in surprise, thinkin' a cloud had come over the moon. But it wasn't a cloud. There were twelve black cats setting in them twelve windows. Every last one of them was staring at Jack with shining eyes.

Jack was real surprised. He probably should have been skeered half to death, but he was a brave feller. He wasn't going to run away from a good job on account of some creepy black cats. He shrugged it off and went back to slicing meat. Why should he care if twelve black cats wanted to keep 'im company?

THE CAT'S PAW

Jack put the meat into the skillet and started cooking it over the fire. Gravy filled up the bottom of the pan and the meat sizzled. It smelled s'good Jack's stomach took to growling. One by one, he turned the strips of meat with his silver knife so they cooked nice and even.

Jack had most forgot about them black cats, until he heard one of them jump down from its window. When he looked up from the skillet, a black cat near as big as a 'coon was setting right next to him. It stretched its paw toward the skillet, meowing: "Sooop dollll."

The words sent a shiver down Jack's spine. They sounded like a black magic spell. He knew "sop" meant to soak something in gravy. And "doll" was the word his old granny used for a person's soul. He realized this black cat had come here to poison the gravy in his pan so it could kill him dead and take away his soul.

Jack jerked the skillet out of reach and glared at the black cat. He wasn't going to be poisoned by some foul magic critter like them other fellers that worked the mill. "Keep yer durned paw away from my meat," he said, shaking the silver knife at the black cat. "You sop in my skillet and I'll cut yer paw off."

The black cat's glowing eyes narrowed in rage. It drew back and glared at Jack. The eleven black cats behind it stirred on their windowsills. Jack ignored them all and kept cooking his food.

"Sooop dollll," the cat mewled again. It reached for the skillet with a huge paw. Jack jerked the pan away and pointed the silver knife at the creature. It bared its long teeth at him. "I told you not to sop yer paw in my meat. You try it again, I'll take it off."

The cat hissed at him. Jack gave it a vicious smile, baring all his teeth. It was Jack against the cat, and he planned to win this fight. The black cat switched its long tail and its eleven followers hissed in unison. Jack ignored them all. He put some meal and seasonings into the pan and stirred everything around until he had a thick gravy. His meal was ready to eat.

Suddenly, the big ol' black cat sprang forward and sopped its foot in Jack's gravy. "Sooop dollll," it howled in triumph.

Skeered for his soul, Jack slashed down with his knife and cut the black cat's paw off. The foot tumbled into the skillet. The black cat screamed and leapt toward the open window. The other cats yowled in panic and every last one of 'em vanished before Jack could turn himself around.

"You done ruined my dinner," Jack shouted after them. He threw the tainted meat and gravy into the fire. When the black cat's paw hit the flames, it turned into a woman's hand.

"Gosh Almighty," Jack swore, knocking the hand from the fire. There was a fancy wedding ring on one finger. He wondered who it belonged to. Jack wrapped the severed hand in paper and put it in a safe spot. Then he scoured his skillet real good to get the poison out before he cooked up another portion of meat for his supper. He didn't think the black cats would return.

In the morning, Jack heard the owner calling to him from the mill yard.

"I figured you was dead," the owner said when Jack came out to meet him. "I'm sure glad to be wrong."

"They tried, but I'm a hard feller to kill," Jack said, and told the owner the whole story.

When Jack showed him the woman's hand with the ring, the mill owner liked to faint. "That's my wife's hand," he gasped. "I gave 'er that ring nearly twenty years ago."

Jack felt terrible for the mill owner. There was only one kind of person that could change themselves into a black cat. And that was a witch.

"I knew she was a-going out sometimes at night to meet with some ladies in the valley. But I never imagined they was the coven of witches that was plaguing our village," the mill owner said. "My wife was ailing this morning and didn't get out of bed. It must be on account of her severed hand. She asked me to send for her friends to give 'er some comfort. They're probably meetin' at my place right now."

Jack and the owner walked to the house to check on the witches. Sure enough, the members of the coven were all there meeting with their ailing leader. The miller sent Jack back to work at the mill and then he went inside with the severed hand to talk to his wife.

About an hour later, a young 'un came running down from the cove, shouting for everyone standing in line at the mill to come quick. The mill owner's house was on fire. By the time they reached the house, it was too late. The fire was burning so hot and so fast no one could put it out. It burned up all twelve witches and the mill owner too. Jack figured that the owner must have set the fire himself to kill off that coven of witches, and probably stayed with them as penance since it wasn't right for him to kill his own wife.

Once the witches were gone, folks in the cove finally started prospering. As for Jack? I heard he got himself a pretty wife and is still working that mill. Makes a good living and has a passel of young 'uns to pass it on to. So, everything turned out just fine.

16

The Bleeding Horse

DEEP CREEK/BRYSON CITY, NORTH CAROLINA

Granny Brown was a light sleeper, so when a muffled scream came from her son's house, it woke her immediately. She sat up in bed and listening intently. She could hear her son and daughter-in-law whispering to one another, and then the night grew silent. She lay back on her pillow and wondered what dream had disturbed Martha's sleep. It would have to be something dire to upset her placid daughter-in-law.

Granny was not surprised when Martha stopped by her house midmorning while she was weeding her garden. Her daughter-in-law was pale and there were dark rings under her eyes from interrupted sleep. She set down her basket and knelt in the next row to weed with her mother-in-law. After working in silence for many minutes, Martha said: "Mother Brown, I had a vision last night."

Granny took note of the wording. A vision, not a dream.

"A foretelling?" she asked.

"I don't know," Martha said. Her hands started shaking so bad she gave up weeding and sat back on her heels. "I hope not. T'was a bad dream."

She fingered a spring of rosemary and drew in a shuddering breath. Granny waited patiently. She'd had her fair share of visions in her lifetime. Good and bad. It seemed to come as part of her healing gift.

"I saw the young 'uns playing in the meadow by the creek. It's their favorite place t'go after chores are done. And that's where I saw it. By the swimming rock."

"What did you see, Martha?" asked Granny gently.

"T'was a horse. A giant bleeding horse. It didn't have no skin—just raw red muscle and veins writhing as the blood pumped through 'em." Martha swallowed hard, her breath coming faster as she spoke. "That bleeding horse came a-galloping into the meadow where the young 'uns were playing ball. It grabbed up little Chrissie in its teeth and ran away with her. That's when I screamed and woke up."

Martha was clutching the ground so hard she was pulling up Granny's plants. Her mouth twisted like she was going to empty her stomach. Granny thrust some peppermint under her nose to calm her and thought fast.

The bleeding horse. Of all the auguries for Martha to see, it had to be the demon horse. Her Scottish grandmother had taught her about the foul creature. Dreaming of the beast was a foretelling of some terrible tragedy. Her grandmother only knew of one person who'd seen the demon in person and lived to tell the tale. And the man went mad after the encounter.

"Mother Brown?" Martha's voice held a pleading note. "What does it mean?"

"T'was the only time you dreamed 'bout the bleeding horse?" Granny asked.

"Only the one time," Martha confirmed.

THE BLEEDING HORSE

"Then it may be just a warning of some danger hereabouts. Let's keep a careful watch over Chrissie and hope for the best," Granny said.

In Granny's experience, visions of augury happened in threes. If they were careful, maybe they could avoid whatever tragedy was foretold for four-year-old Chrissie. Through the years, the bleeding horse had been a forerunner of many things: Disease, famine, theft, invasion, war, dismemberment, death. Granny did not recite this list for Martha. But when the eyes of the two women met, Martha gave a tiny nod, acknowledging everything that Granny hadn't said.

Martha kept Chrissie close over the next week, giving her chores and making up games that kept her in the yard. As the days passed, her fear faded, and she let the child roam more with her brothers and sisters. They were all instructed to take extra care with their little sister.

The second dream came exactly a month after the first. Martha's screams woke the whole house, and she came running to Granny's place in her nightdress. "It took her right off the back of our wagon," she gasped as the frightened family crowded into Granny's tiny cabin. "It galloped up out of nowhere and snatched her right out of my arms." Even in her frantic state, Martha was careful not to say Chrissie's name aloud. The young 'un was blinking sleepily in her father's arms, her curls all awry from sleep.

"Let's pray to the good Lord to protect this family," Granny said firmly.

They all knelt on the floor and prayed. It was the only comfort they had.

The whole family watched over little Chrissie every moment of the day. She wasn't allowed to go to town in case there was disease about. Her siblings took turns playing in the yard so she wouldn't go near the stream. She sat between her parents in the front of the wagon when they went to church on a Sunday. Everything they could think to do to protect the child was done.

When a second month passed without incident, Granny stayed awake all night waiting for a third dream. No one stirred in her son's house, and when dawn came Granny drew in a breath of relief. Maybe their prayers and their care had done it. Maybe they'd broken the demon's augury.

Just then, Martha waved out the bedroom window at Granny, her face alight with hope. "No dream, Mother Brown," she called.

The whole family was cheerful that morning, singing and laughing as they went about their summer chores. It was a hot day and the boys went to play ball next to the swimming hole while the girls rolled a hoop in the yard. Martha and Granny were harvesting herbs in the garden when one of the girls came running.

"Ma, we can't find Chrissie. Come quick. We stopped to pump some water, and all of a sudden she weren't there no more."

"Did you search the house?" Martha demanded, her eyes frantic.

"And the barn," her daughter panted. "Want me to go for Pa? He's out in the field."

"Run find your pa," Martha said. "Granny and I will check the swimming hole. Hurry!"

Martha raced out of the yard with Granny puffing at her heels. They ran down the path toward the swimming hole, and as they burst out of the trees, a huge bleeding horse reared up in the center of the meadow. The raw muscles gleamed red in the sunlight, veins and arteries writhing as the blood pumped through them. The foul stench of sulfur swirled over them as the bleeding horse laughed dementedly. Then it whirled and arrowed toward the big rock by the creek.

"Chrissie," Martha screamed. She hurled herself after the demon and Granny followed as best as her old legs would allow.

Granny heard the boys shouting and a little girl's frightened cry, suddenly cut off by a thud and splash. But all she could see was the bleeding horse rearing up over the swimming rock. And then it vanished with a bang and the smell of sulfur.

Down by the creek, the boys were screaming, but Granny didn't hear Martha's voice at all. She knew in her heart what that meant. She hurried to the edge of the bank beside the swimming rock and looked down. Little Chrissie lay on the sharp stones at the edge of the stream, her small head twisted at an unnatural angle. She'd fallen from the swimming rock and broken her neck. Martha and the boys were stumbling toward her as fast as they could over the wet, loose stones, but Granny knew it was too late. Little Chrissie was dead, just as Martha's visions foretold.

17

The Last Laugh

I was miserable. It was raining, I was wet clear through, and I was lost. Hopelessly lost. My horse plodded along a remote mountain trail that didn't look like a human had set foot on it forever and most of the critters hereabouts avoided it too. So much for my grand fishing vacation in the Smoky Mountains. I couldn't believe I'd gotten lost on my very first day.

Somewhere around dusk, my horse and I entered a rocky gorge whose beauty I might have appreciated in broad daylight but which I cursed now as the high walls cut off the last of the light.

I cursed under my breath as we slowly rode deeper into the gorge. I may as well call it a day and find someplace to camp for the night. I'd need daylight and a tall peak to give me some idea where in heck I was.

Sunk as I was in gloom, I was astonished when I heard a sudden hearty laugh echoing off the walls of the gorge. It was rapidly followed by the sound of voices talking merrily, and then more laughter. I sat up in the saddle, my heart racing with excitement. There were people here! Probably hunters or trappers, I guessed. They must be setting up camp for the evening. They would have a warm fire and food. And a tent to keep off the rain. And directions to get me back home!

"Come on, Brownie old boy, let's find those hunters," I called to my horse, giving him a tap to get him started.

The voices were just ahead of me. Brownie broke into a trot along the narrow path, as eager as I to end our journey in such merry company. We turned onto a side trail that led into a cove. Above the soft hissing of the rain, I could hear the merry voices echoing among the rocks of the gorge. I urged Brownie to a fast gait, and we hastened toward the sound.

Suddenly, the merry laughter came from behind us. We must have missed a turnoff in the trail. Cursing the twilight that made it almost impossible to see, I guided Brownie to a wide, muddy spot and we turned around. I rode back toward the laughing voices, but when we emerged near the stream, there was no campfire, no people, no tents. And yet, I could still hear the echo of voices coming from all sides, punctuated by laughter.

What was going on?

It felt like Brownie and I were in the middle of a crowd of merrymakers. But there was no one in the gorge with us. No one at all. I felt cold sweat beading up all over my body. My heart was hammering against my ribs. Beneath me, Brownie trembled with fear.

After a moment, the sounds died away. All was silent. Even the chuckling of the stream over the rocks in its bed was muted. There was no wind. No rustling in the trees and bushes. No birdcalls or animal noises. The drizzling rain whispered all around us, creating a gray curtain in the twilight. For a moment, I saw shapes in the mist. But they quickly faded.

THE LAST LAUGH

The uncanny stillness was worse than the voices. It felt like the whole world was holding its breath, waiting for something. Then the laughter started again, high pitched and merry. But the merriment was at the expense of others. Now it was a cruel sound, a mockery. The laugher was a mask for something dark and evil. Behind the mocking laughter, another sound was growing. It roared like the raging of the sea in the midst of a storm.

Brownie panicked. I couldn't blame him. He reared, almost unseating me. Then he broke into a gallop, racing for the entrance to the cove as if pursued by the devil himself. I bent low over his neck and held on for dear life.

All around us, the mocking voices shouted and jeered. The menacing laughter echoed from all sides. The roaring grew louder and closer every second. Brownie wheeled onto the main track through the gorge as the mocking voices turned to screams and wails. I desperately wanted to clap my hands over my ears, but I was hanging on for dear life as Brownie fled out of the gorge at top speed.

We were more than a mile out of the gorge before the last of the menacing laughter and terrifying screams died away. Brownie slowed immediately, wrung out from the horrible race. I flopped down onto his mane, too wrung out to stay upright in the saddle as rain drizzled down on my body. I was still tired and wet and miserable, but I didn't care. Brownie and I had made it out of the haunted gorge, and that was all that mattered.

"Thanks for saving us back there, Brownie. I owe you." I gasped. "Find us someplace safe to camp, boy. We both deserve a rest."

Brownie lifted his head and sniffed the air. Then he walked confidently into the inky blackness, following some smell my nose was not keen enough to catch.

I nearly pitched out of the saddle when Brownie stopped in front of a remote cabin deep in the Smoky Mountains. It was so dark I could barely see past my horse's ears. I had no idea how he found this place in the dark. But boy howdy was I glad he did. The warm smell of woodsmoke filled the air, and the flickering light of a lantern in the window gave me hope that my drizzling wet misery was almost at an end. I slid out of the saddle and had to grab hold of Brownie's mane, my legs were shaking so badly. When my strength returned, I hobbled up the single step to the porch and knocked on the door. An old fellow came to greet me and gave me a warm place by the fire. He set me down with a plate of food and his dog for company and went out to feed Brownie and settle him in the barn for a good long snooze.

The kind settler didn't ask any questions that night. He played his fiddle for me while I sat by the fire, trembling, and eating and scratching the ears of his hound dog. He even gave me his bed, insisting on taking a spot next to the fire while I slept in comfort.

Over breakfast the next morning, I told him about my experiences in the haunted gorge. He nodded several times and then told me the following tale.

Not long after the Civil War, a party of young folks decided to spend a few days hunting and fishing in the remote gorge, which had the reputation as a prime spot for both sports. They were overdue by nearly a week when search parties were sent out to find them. The gorge and all the hills around were combed, but there was no sign of the hunting and fishing party. The searchers eventually decided that the group must have been swept away by a flash flood, and the search was abandoned.

Shortly after this, hunters in the vicinity of the lonely gorge began hearing voices and merry laughter echo off the walls of the remote gorge, although no people were present. It was believed that the voices were the spirits of the drowned sportsmen, returned each evening to make merry around the campfire once more.

"It must have been the roaring of the flood I heard, behind the voices and the laughter," I said when the old man finished his tale. "Poor fellows. What a dreadful fate."

After thanking the old man for his hospitality and memorizing the directions that would get me back to civilization, I saddled Brownie and headed down the mountain. We went the long way around to avoid the haunted gorge. Neither Brownie nor I were anxious for another visit. Once was enough.

18

Spear-Finger

CHILHOWEE MOUNTAIN, TENNESSEE

"Uwe la na tsiku. Su sa sai."

The medicine man was meditating before the fire when the sweet voice drifted down to him from the mountaintop. He shivered, for there was a menace within the voice, in spite of the loveliness of its intonation.

The voice came again: "Uwe la na tsiku. Su sa sai."

His mind automatically translated the words: "I eat liver, yum, yum." The medicine man's blood ran cold, for he knew then that he was hearing the voice of the Spear-Finger singing to herself as she made her way toward their village.

At that moment, the voice was drowned by a gust of wind that bent the trees and rattled the bushes. A great flash of lightning ripped through the sky, making the night bright as noon. Thunder shook the whole valley.

The medicine man knew that Spear-Finger was marching down from on high, throwing massive stones between each mountain peak and using them as bridges. Every step she took made the earth shudder and rocks crack. He knew if he hiked to the peak in the morning, he would see footprints sunk deep into the earth under the weight of her stone body. The medicine man hurriedly doused his fire and ran back to the village to warn his chief.

The morning after the storm, runners were dispatched to warn the other villages that Spear-Finger had come to their mountains with her disregard for human life and her taste for liver. Even now, she lurked along the dark pathways and traversed the streambeds, perching in hidden crags and observing the patterns of the people in this new place. She would feed on anyone who strayed too close to her hiding place.

Spear-Finger's body was encased in a stone skin so that no spear could penetrate her flesh, and the forefinger of her right hand was made of a long thin stone that was sharp as a knife and could slice a person open with one flick. And Spear-Finger was a shapeshifter who could take on the guise of a helpless old woman, a young succulent deer, or a craggy warrior.

The men started hunting in groups, and their wives took care to bring their children into their lodges each night. Fear trembled in every heart, for who could protect them if Spear-Finger came to their village? "Stay in the lodge," mothers warned their little ones. "Do not walk alone in the woods, for Spear-Finger is near!"

At first, the children shivered and obeyed. But as the weeks passed with no sign of the monster, the children ceased their vigilance and started playing in the fields outside their village. And so they were unprepared when a sweet old grandmother came hobbling down the path toward them. "Come, my children," she said to them in a gentle voice. "Come let Grandmother brush your hair. It has grown tangled in your games, and your parents will be displeased."

The small daughter of the chief ran to the old lady and sat in her lap. She loved to have her hair combed and submitted to the woman's touch, as the grandmother sang softly: "Uwe la na tsiku. Su sa sai." The child only shuddered a little when the stone finger stabbed through her skin and cut her liver out with a single twist.

When Spear-Finger set the child back on her feet and bade her walk home, the whole world swam oddly before the child's eyes. The little girl took a few steps before falling over dead. By the time she dropped to the ground, Spear-Finger was gone.

The other children had quite forgotten the friendly grandmother who had passed through their field until they found their playmate lying dead. Then they screamed, and the mothers and old men came running, along with a few warriors returned early from their hunt. The little girl was carried with many wails into the village, and the chief and his wife wept in despair.

Back in the woods, Spear-Finger changed shape, disguising herself as a warrior whom she had killed early that morning while he was out hunting. The warrior's wife was completely fooled by the disguise. She left Spear-Finger alone in the lodge that night while she tended the birth of her sister's first child. The monster made short work of the little ones left in her care. By the time the wife returned, her children were dead, their livers gone.

Reeling backward at the gruesome sight, the wife screamed in terror as her neighbors came running to see what was wrong. But there was nothing they could do to comfort her. Spear-Finger had cut her way out of the back of the lodge and disappeared. They found her husband's dead body beside the river and buried him with his children.

SPEAR-FINGER

From that moment, every person who entering the village was suspect—for if the monster could fool the wife of a warrior, who else might she fool? The medicine man was busy day and night performing the magic to confirm all the villagers going about their daily tasks were not Spear-Finger in disguise. Men eyed their wives in suspicion and kept weapons close at hand, and wives refused to leave the children alone with their fathers.

The next morning, two men were sent to set fire to the underbrush in the local grove so the tribe would have easy access to the trees during the harvest. It was a short task that should have taken a single morning. Yet hour after hour passed, and there was no sign of the men's return. Finally, a group was sent to look for them. The bodies of the men were found a few hundred yards into the grove with their hearts crushed and their livers removed. Word of the murder spread like wildfire through the village. Panicking people raced to the lodge of their chief to demand protection from the monster.

Frightened and enraged by the monster who had killed his only child and terrorized his village, the chief called a council of all the surrounding villages and demanded a solution. How could they rid themselves of the Spear-Finger? Many ideas were discussed and discarded before the medicine man proposed that they dig a pit and trap the creature inside. Perhaps then they might examine her close at hand and discover if there was a fatal weakness beneath her skin of stone. No one had a better solution, and so they decided to follow the medicine man's plan.

Under cover of darkness, a large pit was dug on the path outside the village. The next morning, the warriors gathered on either side of the path, hidden among the brush, and a fire was set once again in the chestnut grove. Lured by the cover of the smoke and the promise of fresh liver, Spear-Finger came down from the mountain at speed, hoping to surprise the warriors burning the brush as she had done previously. She slowed when she reached the path to the village and took on her usual disguise of an old woman, hoping to ease the fears of her victims.

As she came hobbling toward the village through the smoke, the warriors gazed at one another in bewilderment. Surely this harmless-looking old woman could not be the fierce monster they had come to trap. But the medicine man gave them a signal: Wait and watch.

The old woman gave a sharp cry of surprise when she stepped onto the brush covering the pit and plummeted to the bottom. Her cry turned into an ear-shattering howl of rage as Spear-Finger realized she had been tricked.

The warriors sprang out from both sides of the path and surrounded the pit, arrows knocked. Below them, a stone-skinned monstrosity with foul locks and a withered brown face leapt about the pit, roaring in anger. Then she reached her sharp stone finger right into the dirt and flicked out a huge rock, which she tossed onto the floor of the pit, followed swiftly by another and then another. She was going to build her way out of the pit! The chief gave the order to fire, and the warriors shot their arrows again and again at the creature, but they bounced uselessly off her stone skin.

Spear-Finger ignored the encircling humans and brushed occasionally at the arrows as if they were no more than bothersome gnats. She kept pulling out stones and piling them into a ramp.

"Poles, spears!" the chief cried when it became obvious that the creature would soon be high enough to climb out of the pit.

Several tribesmen ran into the grove and hacked down long branches to use as poles, while others fetched their spears. They thrust at the Spear-Finger, harrying her and pushing her off the ramp again and again. She gnashed her sharp brown teeth at them and parried their blows with her sharp stone finger, cutting off a few spear tips and nearly decapitating a warrior who leaned too close.

"Pray," the chief ordered his medicine man. "Pray to all the gods for help. If this monster gets out of the pit, we are all dead!"

The medicine man began chanting a prayer, begging the gods to save them from the monster with her stone finger and her lust for blood.

At that moment, a tiny titmouse, still radiant with the glow of heaven, came flying into the midst of the mighty battle, crying "Un un un," the closest it could come to saying "u'na hu," which means heart.

The medicine man gasped: "The heart! Aim for the monster's heart!"

Immediately the warriors notched their arrows and shot the creature in the chest again and again, while others pummeled her with their spears. Spear-Finger laughed at them and climbed further up the ramp, taking a swipe at a warrior with her sharp finger and cutting off his hand.

The warrior fell to the ground and crawled away in an agony of pain. Seeing the glowing titmouse in the brush beside the path, he grabbed it, crying: "Lying creature! See what your lies have caused!" And he cut out part of its tongue. But the titmouse struggled and pecked until he let it go, whereupon it returned to the heavens with only half of its tongue.

"Peace, my brother," said the medicine man as he tended the wound. "The titmouse was right. We must find the creature's heart to kill it. It just didn't know how to tell us where its heart is."

As he spoke, a lovely, glowing chickadee swept down from the heavens and perched for a moment on Spear-Finger's hand, beside the stone finger she used as a knife.

"There," the medicine man cried, understanding the second bird's message. "Aim for the hand! The heart is in the hand!"

Spear-Finger gave a horrible cry when she heard the medicine man's words. She took a swipe at the chickadee, which flew gracefully away. For a moment her palm was exposed, and the men could plainly see the pulsing heart in its center. The chief took aim and sent an arrow right through the creature's heart in memory of his daughter.

Spear-Finger wailed horrifically as she landed among the broken spears and arrows at the bottom of the pit. She twitched several times and then died, her stone finger still waving above her grotesque form. All at once, the monster's dead body turned into a hazy, foul-smelling smoke that whirled around and around before exploding upward, high into the sky, where it disbursed in the wind. And that was the end of Spear-Finger.

19

The Cavern of Skulls

NANTAHALA NATIONAL FOREST, NORTH CAROLINA

There was once a farmer who lived in these here hills who built his settler cabin near a cave. He didn't know the cave was there, until the day the farmer found his old hound dog chewing on a human bone. The farmer took the bone from him and studied it. It looked real old and brittle.

"Where'd you get this old bone?" the farmer asked the dog. The hound sniffed the bone and then set off at a run, eager to find a replacement. The farmer followed his dog through the forest until the dog disappeared behind some shrubbery. When the farmer thrust it aside, he felt a rush of cool air and saw the large mouth of a cave.

When the farmer cautiously followed his hound dog into the cave, he stumbled over a half-buried skull. The farmer gave a shriek of terror, and then laughed at his own foolishness. The person that skull belonged to was long dead. He explored the cavern as far as the light from the entrance would allow, promising himself that he'd come back later with a lantern. He noticed there were a great many skulls piled up inside and decided the cave must have been a burial ground many years before.

Now the polite and respectful thing would have been to leave the old bones where they'd been laid to rest. But the farmer wasn't polite nor respectful when it came to money. He saw the skulls as an opportunity to save some cash. You see, the last time he and his missus went to town, a traveling salesman had been selling a special fertilizer that he claimed would make vegetables grow twice as big. The missus' eyes got real big when he showed her a squash the size of her butter churn. She wanted her husband to buy some of that fertilizer, but the cost was sky high and the farmer said no. The missus had been plaguing the daylights out of him ever since. The farmer figured he could take these old bones and grind them up for fertilizer so his missus would stop her nagging.

"The owners won't mind a bit," he told his hound dog, who was chewing on an arm bone. "They are long gone. And the missus will be right grateful."

So, the farmer got some sacks and filled them up with skulls. Then he hauled them back to his farm in a cart and tumbled them any old how into his shed. Just then, his missus came to the door of the cabin and shouted out that dinner was cooked, so the farmer shut the shed door and went to eat his supper.

"What you got in all those sacks?" asked the missus as she ladled soup into his bowl.

"I got some of that fertilizer you've been hankering for," the farmer said.

The missus squealed with happiness and gave him a smooch that nearly knocked his socks off. What with one thing and another, the farmer didn't get around to grinding down the skulls that evening.

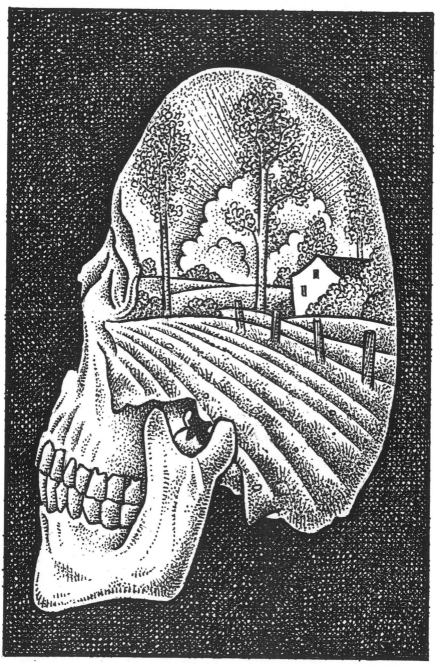

THE CAVERN OF SKULLS

It was as dark and still as any night you'd ever seen in these mountains when the farmer snuggled down in bed to sleep with his missus, who was happier than a young 'un about her fertilizer. He was sleeping sound when a roar like the coming of a big cyclone woke him. The farmer raced to the window, a-fearing the house was going to be swept away. "Margie, get up right now," he shouted. "We gotta get down into the root cellar."

But when the farmer looked outside, the night was calm and still. There were no clouds in the sky. No wind rustling in the trees. He didn't even hear the chirping of the crickets or the rustling of night critters in the bushes. The forest was so quiet it gave him goose bumps. The silence weighed on the farmer as if he were covered in a thick wool blanket. It was hard to breath in the dead air.

The farmer's hands were shaking when he tried to rouse his missus. He needed the sound of her voice to drive away the threatening silence. But his missus wouldn't wake. It was like she was under a some kind of sleeping spell.

The farmer hollered for his hound dog to come, but his voice sounded thin and stretched. It echoed slightly, like he was talking into a tin cup. The sound was strangled by the silence before it was a foot from his body.

The farmer's ears stretched for a noise—any noise. His ears were ringing slightly and he pressed his hands over them, trying to make it stop.

Then the roaring and clacking sound came again, swirling through the silence but not eclipsing it. The farmer staggered to the window, expecting the roof to come off at any second, ripping him and his missus into the gaping maw of the cyclone. What he saw was more terrifying than a storm.

Surrounding his cabin was a band of shadow figures, circling and whirling like autumn leaves. They wailed into the deadened silence. Each individual voice was faint and tinny, but together they made the cyclone sound that first woke him. Red witch lights appeared and disappeared among the shadowy band. Every revolution of the massive circle brought the spirits a foot closer to the house. It would not be long before the ha'nts burst through the walls and claimed the lives of the farmer and his missus.

"Hits the spirits of them old skulls," the farmer gasped. "They've come to get me!"

The wails of the dead grew louder. Red spirit lights flashed brighter than fireworks. The farmer clapped his hands to his head, afraid the screeching would drive him mad. He dropped to his knees and started praying, hoping the holy words would keep the ha'nts at bay.

The unearthly roar continued until first light rimmed the horizon. When at last it faded, the fearful farmer staggered to his feet and ran outside to the shed. He piled the sacks full of skulls into his cart and brought them straight back to the cave, where he laid them out all respectful and proper. Then he blocked up the entrance with brush and stones so his hound dog couldn't get in and steal any more bones.

When he got home, the farmer found his missus cooking breakfast with the hound dog begging for scraps at her feet. He gave a sigh of relief when he realized everything was back to normal.

His missus looked up from her cooking with a twinkling smile, still tickled that he'd bought her the special fertilizer. Then her eyes bulged, and she shouted: "What happened to ya? You've done gone old!"

The farmer stared at her blankly, then looked down at his hands. They were gnarled up and pitted with age. When he looked at his reflection in the mirror, he saw that his hair had turned snow white.

20

Skinned Tom

My buddies and I, we grew up hearing the story of Skinned Tom. Kids told the story at school around Halloween, parents used it to warn us away from lover's lanes when we hit puberty, and so on. It was *the* legend to tell anyone on their first visit to East Tennessee.

When I was ten, I thought it would be cool to frighten my dad's sister, who came to spend Christmas with our family. On Christmas Eve, I told her the story of Skinned Tom and even sang the song for her: "*Have you seen the ghost of Skinned Tom? Long white bones with the skin all gone.*" Over the next few day, I would whisper Skinned Tom's name in the hallways at night when my aunt was getting ready for bed. I thought it was funny to see her jump and spin around. On New Year's Eve, I crept outside after everyone had gone to bed and sang the Skinned Tom song under her window. My aunt screamed so loud she woke my folks, and she made my dad drive her to the airport right then and there. My parents were furious with me, especially when they realized that we'd all have to fly to her home in Texas from now on to celebrate the holidays. My aunt vowed never to return, and she hasn't stepped foot on Tennessee soil since that day.

According to legend, Tom was a handsome fellow who lived in East Tennessee back in the 1920s. He was a rogue with a smooth manner that turned a lot of women's heads. Tom was a traveling salesman, a real love-them-and-leave-them sort. He'd swoop into a new town and sweetheart all the eligible girls, and some not-so-eligible too, if you get my drift. Tom's ardor was intense while he pursued a girl. He'd sweep her off her feet with kisses and flowers, candy and false promises. But once he won her heart, he dropped her like a hotcake and started chasing the next girl in line. Folks claimed he bewitched the girls with some kind of charm. And it certainly seemed that way. The girls would walk around in a daze, falling into daydreams right in the middle of a conversation.

Of course, Tom was as unpopular with the fellows and fathers as he was popular with the girls. There was usually a string of last-minute weddings shortly after Tom left town. Many a bouncing baby that followed in the wake of these impromptu matrimonies looked more like Tom than the man who married the girl.

All the bad karma came home to roost the day Tom met a lovely married woman that we will call "Geraldine." Now Geraldine prided herself on being a virtuous wife and a good mother. But none of that mattered once Tom came courting. The more she spurned his advances, the more persuasive he grew. Geraldine found herself yearning for things she shouldn't.

It didn't take long before the two started meeting "accidentally" in shops and restaurants, and then taking rides in

Tom's fancy motorcar. They became very well acquainted with all the remote places around the town, but their favorite place to canoodle was the local lover's lane.

It wasn't long before they were spotted by the very worst gossip in town, who went straight to Geraldine's husband to tell all. Now Geraldine's husband was the trusting sort, and he just could not believe that his wife would betray him. He was determined to witness the truth for himself before confronting his wayward wife. So he invented a business trip that would take him out of town for a week. Then he checked into a local hotel and kept watch on his wife, following her wherever she went. Once the children were safely packed off to school, it wasn't long before Tom arrived in his fancy motorcar and Geraldine tripped out merrily to meet him.

Geraldine's husband was devastated. He followed the couple at a distance and saw Tom park the car in the local lover's lane and turn toward Geraldine with an amorous eye. At once, his sorrow turned to a terrible rage that made the world go blood red at the edges of his vision. He slammed out of his truck, stalked over to the car and jerked open the driver's door. Untangling Tom from his wife, he threw the salesman from the car while his Geraldine desperately begged him for mercy.

When her gaze met that of her husband, Geraldine realized he was too far gone for mercy. She flung herself out the passenger side door and fled half-clothed into the woods. Behind her, Tom screamed for mercy as Geraldine's husband pulled a hunting knife from his belt and started surgically slicing off his skin, one long strip at a time. Tom's screams became muted and ceased long before the husband was through. He tossed the bloody but

SKINNED TOM

still-breathing salesman on the ground and draped the man's skin on the open car door. Then he marched into the woods to look for Geraldine.

Later that evening, Geraldine's husband turned himself in to the police for murder and sent them to the lover's lane to retrieve the bodies of Tom and Geraldine. When they arrived, they found blood everywhere, and Tom's skin hanging from the open car door. A quick search revealed Geraldine in the woods nearby. She was bleeding from several knife wounds but miraculously still alive. But Tom's skinless body had disappeared.

Ever since that day, the spirit of Skinned Tom has stalked all the local lover's lanes in East Tennessee, seeking out cheating couples and dismembering them with the same knife that was once welded against himself.

Now, I wasn't thinking about Skinned Tom or much of anything but romance on the night Justine and I parked the car in a secluded lane on the outskirts of town. I'd met her at a bar, and we'd been flirting outrageously for more than a week. When she suggested going for a drive, I totally knew what she wanted. And I had no objections. If things worked out the way I planned, I'd soon be taking Ms. Justine home to meet the folks. She was totally my type.

We were just getting cozy when someone thumped the back of the car so hard it shook. There were no lights in that dark lane, and no headlights had passed us coming or going.

"What is that? Is it a bear?" Justine gasped, pulling away from me and looking in alarm out the back window.

From outside the car, I caught a wisp of song: "*Have you seen the ghost of Skinned Tom? Long white bones with the skin all gone . . .*"

"It better not be some eavesdropping local kid," I muttered, flustered and disoriented by the interruption and the eerie chant still wafting faintly through the closed window.

I was straightening my clothes when my door was jerked open and I was thrown from the car by an icy wind. I rolled over just in time to avoid being stabbed with a hunting knife. I gazed up at a gruesome, skinless figure that glowed with a fiery light as it slashed at me with its knife. I screamed.

Justine was suddenly beside me, pulling me upright and shouting at the ghost of Skinned Tom: "I'm getting a divorce, all right? It will be finalized in the morning. *He didn't know!*"

She pepper sprayed the ghost, but Skinned Tom didn't even blink. He took another swing with the knife, which seemed much too solid to be supernatural. We didn't wait around. Flinging ourselves into the car, we peeled out of the lover's lane so fast we could smell the tires.

When we were safely in the parking lot behind my building, I looked over at Justine. She was pale and shaking with nerves. "I should have told you about the divorce," she gasped. "I never thought making out with you would trigger the ghost of Skinned Tom. I should have known better. My granny warned me long ago that there was an evil spirit haunting the area and that it became enraged when anyone was caught philandering in its sphere."

"I didn't think it was real," I said. My voice sounded too high pitched to belong to me, but it reflected how I felt. "Thanks for saving me back there."

"I think maybe we should wait until my divorce is final before we . . . you know," Justine said.

"I agree," I said. "Can I drive you home?

"I'd like that. Thank you," she said primly. We held hands as I drove and I gave her a chaste kiss on the cheek at her door.

Back in my apartment, I realized that I owed my aunt an apology letter. She'd been right to fear the ghost of Skinned Tom. I would be more respectful of spooky old legends from now on. I'd finally learned my lesson.

21

The Scale

CHEROKEE, NORTH CAROLINA

There is a tale told of two brothers who went hunting in a lonely part of the mountains. When they made camp for the night, one brother built a fire and created a bark shelter while the second made his way up the creek, searching for a deer to shoot for their evening meal.

The woods were strangely silent as the young hunter crept along a narrow deer path. He strained his ears for a telltale rustle, but the whole forest held its breath, as if trying to escape the notice of a terrible predator. Suddenly, a great noise reverberated from the mountain top. It sounded as if two giant animals were fighting one another in the vicinity of a remote mountain pass.

The hunter gripped his weapons and slid stealthily through the underbrush, wondering what creatures might cause such a loud commotion. When he reached the pass, he beheld a massive snake as round as a tree trunk covered with fiery scales. A pair of horns rose out of its crested head and on its forehead was a magic crystal as clear as a mountain stream with one red streak piercing it from top to bottom. The hunter gasped in fear, for this was Uktena, a monster so dangerous that its breath was poison and its crystal magic.

The giant crested snake had wrapped its coils around a massive warrior dressed in silvery clothes that shimmered like lightning. The warrior fought bravely with knife and spear, but the giant snake was slowly strangling him.

The hunter crouched in the shrubbery as man and snake fought. The fiery blaze of the magic crystal riveted his attention. He found himself swaying back and forth in the manner of a serpent, spellbound by the monster. Little flames of fire puffing from the serpent's mouth added an eerie red and orange glow to the otherworldly scene.

The constricted warrior caught sight of the young hunter and gasped: "Nephew, I am dying. Help me defeat the Uktena. For he is also *your* enemy."

His words woke the hunter from his thrall. What had he been thinking to neglect his uncle in this manner? And yet, what could he do? Only one man, a great magician from long ago, had ever killed an Uktena. Though he had heard the story numerous times, in this critical moment his mind was a blank. How had the magician defeated the great serpent?

Then it came to him. The hero had put an arrow through the seventh ring of color behind the snake's mighty crest, where it kept its heart. The hunter lifted his bow and aimed at the monster. Praying that he had accurately remembered his teaching, the hunter fired his arrow at the massive Uktena.

The arrow flew true and struck the mighty serpent in the center of the seventh circle, piercing its heart. Noxious smoking blood spurted from the wound. The Uktena swayed dizzily and its coils loosened. The silver-clad warrior fell out of its grip, twisting in midair and landing on his feet in front of the young hunter.

"Quickly nephew," the warrior gasped. "The danger has not passed!"

With a jolt of fear, the hunter realized he was correct. In the old tale, the dying Uktena had spewed venom all over the mountains. The magician had only survived by hiding away inside a pit surrounded by magical fire. But there was no pit at the mountain pass and the hunter was no medicine man with the ability to conjure magic flames.

The warrior gave a mighty shout that disoriented the writhing serpent. It flailed and slithered along the ridge, perilously close to the edge of the cliff. The hunter sprang out of the shrubbery and added his own war cries to the warrior's bellows. The Uktena was billowing flame, its crystal flashing with white and red light as it thrashed in agony. It shrank away from the echoing cries, rearing up in agony as it hissed out its poison.

The warrior flung himself against the hunter, knocking the young man to the ground to avoid the poisonous puff of breath. The Uktena tried to coil itself, lost its balance, and tumbled over the edge of the cliff. Its massive body knocked over trees and great stones as it rolled down the mountain, raising dust and debris in a thunderous landslide.

The two men rose shakily to their feet and stared down into the valley. A wide swath of uprooted trees, razed bushes, and tumbled boulders delineated the path of the dying monster. Little venom fires burned along the trail of destruction, the foul smoke killing all the vegetation in the vicinity.

The young hunter stared appalled at the destruction. Thick red blood was pooling around the crested head of the snake, which twitched along its massive length a few times before its eyes glazed over in death.

THE SCALE

"It will take some time for the poisoned blood and venom breath to boil off," the warrior said casually. "We will have to wait here until then. I'll summon the creatures to help."

The warrior raised his silver-clad arms and called in a language known only to spirits. Immediately, great clouds of insects and birds descended into the stricken valley and landed upon the Uktena, devouring the monster down to its bones.

The young hunter gaped in awe at his companion. This man was not mortal. His clothes were the silver-white of lightning, his knife and spear were already restored to pristine condition.

"Who are you?" the young hunter asked, though he already knew.

"You may call me 'Man of the Lightning,'" the warrior said, motioning for the young hunter to sit with him on a pair of boulders near the pass. "You have helped me, and I wish to give you a gift. I have a medicine that will ensure that you never again lack for game."

"I seek no reward," the young hunter said modestly, but he knew better than to argue with a being such as the Man of the Lightning.

They passed the time in conversation, watching the great snake vanish under the hungry mouths of the birds and insects. When darkness fell, the two men walked along the path of destruction until they reached the bones of the great serpent. Motioning the young hunter to stand back, Man of the Lightning went to the head and carefully wrapped the magic crystal into a deerskin and placed it in his pouch. "This is too strong a medicine for you," he told the young hunter, who nodded his agreement. He wouldn't have touched the crystal if his life depended upon it.

Man of the Lightning scanned the ground beneath the bones of the Uktena and pointed to a spot that glowed just under the earth. The two men dug until they reached the glowing object, which was a single scale left from the body of the great serpent.

Man of the Lightning scraped twigs from a nearby tree which had once been struck by lightning. Using the power leftover from the thunderstorm, he created a magical fire with the twigs and tossed the scale into it. When the scale had burned down to a single coal, Man of the Lightning removed it from the fire and wrapped it up in a deerskin. Giving the scale to the hunter, he said: "As long as you carry this medicine bundle with you, you will never lack for game. But do not bring it into your shelter tonight, for your brother is near death from the venomous breath of the Uktena and the magic of the scale would overwhelm him. When you reach camp, hang the medicine bundle from a tree and add shavings from this cane to some water. When your brother drinks the water, it will make him well again."

Man of the Lightning gave the medicine bundle and a piece of cane to the hunter. Then he vanished in a flash of light before the young man could thank him.

The young hunter returned to his camp and carefully placed the medicine bundle on a tree outside the shelter. Then he mixed shavings from the cane into some water and used the medicine to cure his dying brother.

The young hunter told few about his meeting with Kanati, the Great Thunderer, for who would believe such a tale? But ever after, whenever he searched for game, the young hunter always found it. So, his family never went hungry, even in the leanest of years.

22

I'll See You in Hades

ELKMONT

GREAT SMOKY MOUNTAINS NATIONAL PARK

You could have knocked me over with a feather when my cousin Tim walked in my door one winter's evening. I had just settled down in front of the fire with a glass of moonshine when he sashayed into the house, as cool as you please.

Tim looked pretty good for a man that had been dead for nigh on a month. His Sunday-go-to-meeting clothes glowed with a pale blue light and his face was the same as I remembered, though the features sometimes twisted to one side or another in a manner that made my skin crawl. There was a long chain tied around his waist and that dragged across the floor with an eerie scraping sound that made my teeth ache.

Tim paced up and down the room, with the chain rattling behind him. I took a long swallow of moonshine to calm my nerves and said: "What in tarnation are you doing here, Tim? Aren't you supposed to be in heaven?"

Tim's face did one of those swooshy movements where his eyes and mouth traded places with his ears and nose. When his face came right way round, he gave a sigh that made my hair stand on end. "Ohhhhhh," Tim moaned. "They turned me away from heaven, Pete me lad. They said I have unfinished businesssssssssss. . . ." The final syllable turned into a hiss of despair, and Tim's ghost rose a good two feet off the floor. His body filled with dark shadows that spiraled underneath his skin.

I gulped some more moonshine. This was no time to be sober. "What was your unfinished business?" I asked once the phantom had calmed down a mite.

"Yooooou remember how I passed?" Tim groaned.

"It's rather hard to forget," I said dryly.

My cousin had dropped dead in Widow O'Rourke's yard during an argument over a pig. According to the widow, Tim lost a bet to her husband and refused to make good on it when he learned that Mr. O'Rourke had been killed in a logging accident shortly thereafter. The widow told my cousin to produce the contested sow at once or else she'd set the law on him. Tim swore up and down that he hadn't made any bet and the two of them started shouting at each other so loud that everyone in earshot came running to see what it was all about.

Finally, Tim yelled: "I'll see you in Hades before I'll give you a pig!" And then he dropped dead, just like that. The doctor said his heart gave out from all the shouting and stress.

"The Widow O'Rourke was riiiiiight," Tim's spirit said sadly. "I owed her a pig. When her husband passed, I thought I could weasel out of the debt. But I was wrong. When I got to heaven, they turned me away. They tied this chain around my waist and sent me to wander the earth until my debt was paid."

That didn't seem quite right to me. Maybe Tim owed the widow a pig, but she had aggravated him to death. It seemed like she was more in the wrong than my cousin. But there was

I'LL SEE YOU IN HADES

no use arguing with heaven. They'd sent my cousin back to earth in chains, and that was that.

"So how do you set things right?" I asked.

"I need your help," Tim groaned. "I cannot drive a pig in my spirit form. You must come with me to fetch it and take it to the Widow O'Rourke. Then I will be free."

The phantom held out his hand and I gingerly took it. It felt like I was touching ice. My body went all thin and airy, and when the ghost rose up through the roof of my cabin, I rose with him as if my body were no longer a solid presence. We sailed through the frost-bitten air until we reached a small clearing where a herd of wild pigs had snuggled down for the night. Tim set me down by the pigs and pointed to a fat sow sleeping on the edge of the herd.

"Hold out your hand to that sow and she will follow you," my cousin instructed.

That wasn't normal pig behavior, but Tim had evidently gained some supernatural powers during his month of wandering. As soon as I held my hand out to the pig, she woke with a happy grunt and followed me like a pet dog.

We were miles from the Widow O'Rourke's place, and it was quite late when I knocked on her door.

"Who's a-knocking there?" came a sleepy voice through the closed door.

"It's Peter Donnelly, Widow O'Rourke," I said politely. "I have a delivery for you."

"A bachelor like yourself shouldn't be interrupting a poor widow's sleep in the middle of the night," she replied. "But you've a good reputation, so I'll open the door to you. Just give me a moment to put on a shawl."

A moment later, the door swung wide and the Widow O'Rourke peered out with her lantern.

"I suppose you should come in," she began, but broke off when she saw Tim's ghost hovering beside me.

"What the devil did you bring to my house, Peter Donnelly?" she cried in surprise.

"Tis me, what was Tim Sullivan in life," my cousin explained. "I have come to pay my debt. Here is the pig I owed you."

The widow raised her lantern higher and saw the wild sow waiting placidly at my heels. When she looked back at my cousin Tim, her face was bright red with rage.

"You brought me a wild sow, Tim Sullivan? You cheater! You promised me husband yer prize sow. Death hasn't changed ye. Yer still a rascal and a liar."

"No such thing! The bet never said what kind of sow t'would be," roared the ghost. "You are trying to cheat my poor widow out of her prize sow, just like you cheated me out of my life." He glared at the Widow O'Rourke, his body throbbing between blue light and dark shadow. "I have brought you this fine sow in payment of my debt and I am quit of me promise. Will you take it?"

"You ain't quit of yer promise until I say you are," shouted the Widow O'Rourke. "I'll see you in Hades afore I'll take that wild sow."

"I will take you at your word, Widow O'Rourke," shouted my cousin's ghost. "Hades it is!"

The phantom threw his chain around the widow and flew straight up into the sky, carrying the shrieking woman away with him.

I blinked several times in shock and then looked down at the pig. "Well, that was an interesting end to an interesting evening. Shall we go home?" The wild sow watched with interest as I picked up the fallen lantern and politely shut the door. Then she followed me home, where I served us both a round of moonshine. I think we both deserved it.

23

SWAIN COUNTY, NORTH CAROLINA

Bertha was not my favorite relative. She was bold as brass, with a sharp tongue and a bullying manner that did not endear her to me. Worse, she turned coy and sweet around boys and adults, hiding her true colors behind a false front. So when she moved in with my family after her folks passed, I was not pleased. Bertha was older than the rest of us, and she bossed us around something cruel. Mama saw through her conniving, but Papa was completely taken in.

All us girls shared a room, and Bertha and I had to sleep in the same bed. I ended up with twelve inches of space and Bertha took the rest. Anytime I tried to claim more territory, she'd kick me until I moved, pretending all the while that she was fast asleep.

As soon as I was old enough, I got work in the local mercantile. The owners offered to provide room and board as well as my wage, so I stayed in town during the week and went home for Sunday dinner. It was a relief to get away from Bertha, but I couldn't figure out why she didn't take the job herself. It was a fine opportunity for a girl from a poor family, but Bertha let the position go to me. I figured she preferred bossing the young 'uns over doing an honest day's work. But it turned out, she had something else in mind.

Folks shopping at the mercantile started gossiping about Bertha and the preacher's boy. He'd been going with a girl named Bess for nearly a year but dropped her as soon as Bertha looked his way. Lord Almighty, I was furious. Bess was a nice girl and didn't deserve to be thrown over for someone like Bertha.

I heard that Bess was heartbroken and had pleaded with Bertha to let the preacher's son go. Bertha, of course, had refused. There was some speculation that Bess might be in the family way, so devastated was she by the whole situation.

Before a month had passed, Bertha and the preacher's boy were engaged to wed. Her future papa-in-law looked embarrassed when he made the announcement on Sunday. Bess started crying softly into her handkerchief and her mama took her away. Her granny, who was the town herbalist and healer, sat stiff and disapproving in the pew, glaring at the preacher and his son. But she turned all soft and sweet when she met Bertha in the churchyard after the sermon.

"Congratulations to ye," she said, taking Bertha's hand into her gnarled grip. "I'm making ye a quilt for yer new household."

Bertha smirked and tossed her blond curls. "That is right kind of you, Granny," she said and winked at me over the old lady's shoulder.

Two weeks later, Granny brought a pink and green quilt to church with her and presented it to Bertha. "The pattern's called Catch My Breath," Granny told Bertha. "It's a wedding quilt, so you must sleep under it every night to dream of your true love. And it will add spice to the marriage bed, if'n you know what I mean."

THE CURSE

Bertha cooed over the quilt and showed it to everyone, including Bess. When we got home after church, she went right to our room and tucked it carefully on her side of the bed.

It was a lovely quilt, all soft blues and pinks. I'd never seen the pattern before. It was full of circles and oblongs made out of many small triangles. If you looked at it just right, it looked like a menacing face with an open mouth full of sharp teeth. There was a faint smell of herbs coming from the quilt. I smelled tans, rue, mug wort, and pennyroyal. Those were strange herbs to give to a bride. I shivered suddenly.

"I've never heard of a Catch My Breath quilt," I said. "I still don't understand why Bess's grandmother would give you a wedding quilt."

"She probably invented the pattern just for me," Bertha said smugly, tossing her curls. "And she gave me the quilt so everyone would know I am a much better match for the preacher's son than silly old Bess."

She walked away with her nose in the air. I sighed and went down to help Mama with the Sunday dinner.

I was shocked when I saw Bertha at church the next week. She was pale and there were dark rings under her eyes. Her perky blonde curls were drooping and there were lines around her lips.

"What's wrong with Bertha?" I whispered to Mama during the first hymn.

"She ain't sleeping too good," Mama told me. "Hush now. We'll talk after dinner."

Bertha was her usual bossy self in the churchyard, but I couldn't help noticing that she walked kind of stiff on the way back to the cove.

"She's been having nightmares," Mama told me after dinner as we washed up the dishes. "Says a black cat comes and lays on her chest each night. She wakes up screaming and gasping for breath."

"You don't reckon . . ." I paused, wondering how much to say. Mama raised an eyebrow at me. "You don't reckon it's that Catch My Breath quilt Granny gave her, bringing on the dreams?"

"Pshaw, it ain't nothing of the sort. It's bridal nerves I expect," Mama said. "The wedding's only a few weeks away and there's so much to do to get ready to set up housekeeping. I don't know how we are going to be ready in time."

Mama was right about all the work. Every minute I wasn't at the mercantile, I was sewing napkins for Bertha's hope chest or making lace or running errands. It was a real whirlwind of activity. Bertha didn't seem to be doing much of the work herself, except standing for the fitting for her fancy wedding dress. She seemed paler each time I saw her. The lines on her face grew more pronounced and she held herself at a funny angle as if her back hurt her. Mama said she still had nightmares about a black cat that sat on her chest and pressed the air out of her. A couple of times, Mama found Bertha with her head all wrapped up in the quilt. "It's no wonder she feels like she can't breathe," Mama scolded. "I keep telling her to tuck it in before she goes to sleep at night. But half the time she doesn't remember."

"I think you should take that quilt away from her, Mama," I said. "I think its cursed."

But Mama didn't believe in curses. And Bertha was so proud of that quilt that she wouldn't listen to me when I told her that I thought the quilt was causing the dreams. "You're just jealous.

And you're right to be. I'm getting married and you'll be an old maid," she jeered.

The wedding day arrived and we helped Bertha do her hair up nice. The fancy dress looked real fine, but Bertha wasn't at her best. She was too thin, there was no color in her face, and her curls had lost their bounce. But she was as coy and bossy as ever, and the look of dawning terror on the preacher boy's face when she marched down the aisle and took his arm told me he'd finally realized what he was getting into.

During the wedding supper, I sought out Granny. "Where is Bess?" I asked her. "I haven't seen her in town."

"Bess is staying with her cousin," Granny said. "There's a nice farmer in that village who would make a good husband." And father. Neither of us said it, but we both understood.

I reached into my pocket and pulled out a lace-edged handkerchief that I'd made while I was doing all the extra sewing for Bertha's wedding.

"It's a gift for Bess. I hope everything comes right for her," I said, handing it to Granny.

"I'll be sure she gets it," Granny said. "Thank ye."

We gave Bertha and her new husband a rousing send-off. They were staying in a remote hunting cabin for their honeymoon, before returning to set up housekeeping in a small cabin behind the preacher's house. Bertha took the new quilt with her, since Granny had hinted it would make the marriage bed even sweeter.

No one heard anything from the happy couple for several days. We figured they'd decided to extend their honeymoon, so no one was worried, though more than one ribald remark was made. After a week, the preacher and Papa decided enough was enough. The couple must be getting low on food and you couldn't live on nothing but love and air. They went to the hunting cabin to visit the newlyweds and ask them to come home. When they stepped inside, they found Bertha and the preacher's boy dead on the bed, the wedding quilt wrapped tightly around their throats.

24

The Wayside Inn

HAYWOOD COUNTY, NORTH CAROLINA

Many years ago, a captain headed down from his mountain home with a few head of cattle he hoped to sell for a profit at a city market. The sunny afternoon was soon overtaken by clouds, and by dinner time it was rainy and miserable. The trails were swampy, the creeks swollen, and a mist obscured everything.

It was a wretched business herding cattle in wet weather. When the captain spotted the lights of a lonely wayside inn, he turned his horse off the trail and drove his stock toward the building. The inn loomed menacingly out of the mist as he drew near. There was something sinister about the decrepit building. Its dark windows peered down at him like the eyes of the dead.

What foul secrets resided inside these walls, the captain wondered. He shook off the thought and urged his cattle toward the rear of the wayside inn, where a fenced paddock stood beside a rundown barn. A burly stableman with hard eyes herded the cattle into the paddock and stabled his horse. The captain did not like the greedy look on the man's face, but there was no good place to camp along this section of trail. The inn was the safest place to spend the night.

Once the stock was settled, the captain walked up to the inn to request a room for the night. On his way, he noticed loose earth in several places as if someone had recently filled rather large holes. There seemed no rhyme or reason for the excavations. The captain might have paused to ponder the mystery, but rain was hammering down on him and a strong wind threatened to blow his hat off. He hurried up the steps and across the rickety porch, his arm raised to knock on the weathered door. It opened before he reached it.

A thin man with a scraggly beard and hard eyes welcomed him inside and took his wet overcoat. The captain requested a room for the night and a meal if one was to be had. The man's eyes gleamed when he pulled out a full money belt and paid in advance for both.

The innkeeper directed the captain to a seat by the fire in the small dining room and went to the kitchen to request supper for the new guest. The floor of the dining room was sticky under his boots and the grimy table did nothing to enhance the captain's appetite. He wiped off the worse of the spills with his handkerchief, then sat and steamed by the fire awaiting his meal. The innkeeper's slatternly spouse slammed into the dining room a few minutes later and put a bowl of stew in front of him. She gave him an evil glare when he asked for bread but stomped to the kitchen and returned with a basket. The napkin needed a wash, but the rolls inside were fresh.

While he ate, the captain surreptitiously watched the innkeepers as they patrolled dining room and parlor. He did not like the way the couple exchanged sly glances when they thought he wasn't attending. The captain decided he would lock his door that evening in case the couple decided to steal his money belt.

After his meager meal, the captain was shown an upstairs room at the back of the inn. It was sparsely furnished with a bed, a washstand, and a small wardrobe. A faint stench of decay fouled the air. The captain wrinkled his nose and tossed his pack on the bed. Then he strolled over to the barred window to check on his cattle in the paddock. Behind him, the innkeeper tutted and moved the pack to the wardrobe before bidding him goodnight. As the captain contemplated the possible reasons for the iron bars that were installed on the window, he heard the click of a key turning in the lock. Whirling, the captain hurried to the door. It would not open. His room had just become a prison.

Heart pounding, the captain went to get the pistol out of his pack. It wasn't there. The innkeeper had removed it before he placed the bag into the wardrobe. This did not bode well. The captain had a knife tucked into his boot, but he was not sure how much use it would be if both the innkeepers and the farmhand came for his money belt.

It was not just this thought that nauseated him. The longer he stayed in the room, the stronger grew the stench of decay. What was that foul odor? The captain looked in the wardrobe, but it was empty. Then he dropped down on his knees and glanced under the bed, thinking a rat had perished there. He found himself eyeball to eyeball with a corpse.

The captain gasped and scrambled away; one hand clamped over his mouth to keep from losing his dinner. The corpse's face was bruised and scraped as if he had been violently beaten. Swallowing bile, the captain steeled himself and made a thorough

THE WAYSIDE INN

investigation of the body. Yes, the man had been battered to death. His skull was caved in on one side and several limbs were broken. The corpse looked like it was several days old.

The captain heard footsteps coming up the stairs and several voices were audible. He recognized the rumbling bass of the brutish stableman and the innkeeper's light tenor. "The money belt wasn't in the pack," the innkeeper said. "It must still be on him."

The captain grabbed the corpse and flung it onto the bed. Arranging the bedclothes over the body, he concealed himself against the wall so the door would hide him when it opened. Clutching his knife, he prayed for an opportunity to save himself.

The key clicked in the lock and the door was thrust violently open. Three men rushed inside, armed with axes and knives. They started hacking violently at the corpse in the bed.

While they were thus distracted, the captain slid through the door and scrambled down the stairs. He bolted out the front door, hoping to avoid the woman in the kitchen, and slipped along the sidewall of the inn, eyeing the barn. At first glance, he couldn't see a guard. Taking a risk, the captain slithered through the mud and slid inside. His horse was in the first stall.

There was no time for saddle or bridle. At any moment, they might realize the body wasn't him. He mounted bareback and raced out of the torn-up yard, muddy water splashing up in his wake. Behind him, he heard shouts and curses as the murderers finally realized that the dead man wasn't bleeding, and the money belt was nowhere to be found.

The captain galloped through to the storm to the nearest settlement to report the crime. Officers were immediately sent to investigate, and at dawn the next morning they arrested the murderous innkeeper and his men. A search of the premises revealed multiple graves under the disturbed earth in the yard. The captain's cattle had been hidden in a nearby cove and his saddle, bridle, and pack were buried in the hay loft.

How long the murderous innkeepers had plied their foul trade was anyone's guess. They counted at least eleven graves in the yard and reckoned more were hidden in the hills. But everyone agreed the captain had been very fortunate to escape.

25

Secret Spring

GREAT SMOKY MOUNTAINS NATIONAL PARK

Way back in the day, my great granddaddy knew the very best moonshiner in these hills. Granddaddy always referred to him as "McGill" so no one would be able to identify him or his family, but folks from his generation all knew who he meant.

McGill made moonshine that tasted better than anyone else, and folks said it was on account of the water he used from a secret spring. No one could pry the location out of McGill, and no one could replicate his moonshine. It was in demand in the blind tigers—places that sold illegal alcohol—all over Tennessee and North Carolina.

McGill made a heap of money on his moonshine, but he didn't pay no taxes on it, which put him at odds with the revenuers. They were always trying to pin something on McGill, but none of them could find his secret still or prove the contraband whiskey they captured was his. Folks reckoned there was some kind of magic spell protecting McGill from harm.

Now Granddaddy and McGill were closer than brothers, so one day McGill blindfolded my granddaddy, put him up on a mule, and brought him to the secret still to taste his latest batch o' shine. Granddaddy had to crawl on his hands and knees through a tunnel with briars and bushes stabbing him all which away. He felt plenty battered by the time McGill took off his blindfold.

Granddaddy looked around in amazement at McGill's secret spot. There were impenetrable hedges of laurel and rhododendron all around the clearing. Tall trees shaded the clearing, and a huge rock dominated the western part. A spring bubbled up from under the rock and formed a pool before the water ran in a merry trickle underneath the thicket. The still was set up in the center of the clearing.

"Not even the wild hogs can get in 'ere," McGill boasted with a grin.

He had a fine batch of whiskey waiting in the still. Together, they got it bottled up and ready to sell. Then they sprawled on the big rock and had themselves a round. McGill called it a "taste test."

"This is a real nice spot," my granddaddy said. The trickling spring and the smell of the laurel was soothing, and the hedges made it feel safe and private. Soon, McGill was snoozing with his hat over his eyes and Granddaddy sprawled across the big rock and gazed lazily down into the spring. At first, all he could see was his own reflection. Then a pair of glowing eyes appeared in the depths of the spring. Granddaddy jumped but he couldn't pry his gaze away as the eyes rose toward him. Among the ripples, he could see a long dark hair and a twisted green face with a razor-toothed smile. Clawed hands stretched toward him, as the creature drew near the surface. Granddaddy was terrified. If those hands closed around his throat, he was a goner. But he was paralyzed and couldn't twitch a muscle.

Suddenly, Granddaddy was knocked sidewise away from the spring. He rolled down the back side of the rock and landed in a briar bush. McGill jumped down in front of him, his eyes wide with fear. "Are ya trying to get yerself kilt?" he shouted. "Stay away from that spring!"

Granddaddy's heart was pounding so hard he couldn't hardly talk. He stared up at his best friend, not sure what to say or think. His mind was racing so fast he barely registered all the thorns sticking into him from the briar patch.

"Son of a . . ." Granddaddy swore. "Did you go an' make a deal with the devil to get access to that there haunted spring?"

"It's more of a water spirit, I reckon," McGill said sheepishly. "An' it don't like strangers meddlin' with it. Tries to drown 'em. I got lucky my first time here, beat it back with a big stick and it ain't bothered me since."

Granddaddy scrambled out of the brambles and McGill gave him a hand up.

"It don't aim to spend any more time in this ha'nted spot," he told his friend. "And speakin' as your friend, I don't think it's worth riskin' your life over some whiskey."

"Some *durn great* whiskey," McGill corrected him. "An' hit's my choice to make."

"True enough," said Granddaddy. "Now where'd you put that goldurned blindfold?"

My granddaddy was still shaking in his boots when he got home that night. He couldn't believe his old friend was messing about with a water demon. His old granny had told him many stories about the water spirits. Most promised dire consequences for anyone that encountered one.

SECRET SPRING

It was a good six months after Granddaddy visited the ha'nted spring that McGill disappeared. He missed one moonshine delivery, then two. This wasn't like him, so his niece went up to the old cabin to check on him. He was nowhere to be found. The family searched around some, but they figured he was hiding from the revenuers, so they weren't too worried. But Granddaddy wasn't so sure. He kept dreaming about yellow eyes in the depths of a spring-fed pool.

Now Granddaddy knew in a general way where McGill took him when they visited the ha'nted spring. And he had a knack for wayfinding which he hadn't mentioned when McGill blindfolded him. Out of respect—and gut-numbing terror—he never went back to McGill's secret still. But he knew he could find it again.

Granddaddy saddled up his horse and went way up into the mountains as far as he could ride. After some searching, he found the worn-out spot on a tree that McGill used as a hitching post for his mule. He took a faint deer path until he came to a massive wall of juniper and rhododendron so thick you couldn't see through it. Nothing could get inside that mess. Except McGill.

It took Granddaddy a while to locate the entrance to the tunnel. When he found it, he crawled through with his gun tight in one hand and a knife in the other, not sure what he'd find inside the secret clearing. He hovered just inside the far entrance, scoping out the scene. There was the still full of moonshine. And there was the big rock with the spring bubbling at its foot. Beside it grazed a small horse with a long mane. It raised its head and looked at him with wicked green eyes. Granddaddy knew at once that it was the water spirit.

"Where's McGill?" Granddaddy shouted at the water spirit. The pony smiled at him, baring inhumanly sharp teeth. Then it leaned down and delicately picked up a crumpled object laying at its feet. It was McGill's hat.

"You goldurn monster," Granddaddy cried. "Did ya drown 'im?"

He emerged from the tunnel with his knife and gun at the ready, watching the water demon closely. It dissolved into a gusher of water and reformed as a beautiful maiden. She winked at Granddaddy and dove into the pool.

Granddaddy heard a faint cry from the briar patch behind the rock: "Will, is that you?"

It was McGill.

"It's me," Granddaddy confirmed.

"That water demon's been playing with me like a goldurn cat with a mouse. It's keeping me prisoner in me own still," McGill called. "I had to tie me self to a tree with me own belt to keep from drownin'."

Granddaddy edged his way around the clearing, careful to keep the still between himself and the pool. He found McGill lying behind the big rock, his right arm bound to a low-hanging tree branch. His clothes were in bloody tatters where the kelpie's razor teeth had dragged at him and his face was a mass of bruises and scratches. There were teeth marks all over the belt, and in one place it was nearly bit through.

"Why's it tormenting you?" asked Granddaddy, freeing McGill from the tree branch. "I thought you made a deal."

"The deal was up," McGill said miserably. "I wanted to be the best moonshiner in these hills. I asked it fer ten years of good fortune, and the ten years ended last week."

"And you still came back?" Granddaddy asked incredulously.

"I wanted me last batch of whiskey," McGill said stubbornly. "I started it afore the ten years was up. I figured it still counted as part of the deal."

"The water spirit didn't agree with you," Granddaddy said dryly.

He hustled McGill across the clearing and into the low tunnel. Behind them, the water horse screamed as Granddaddy deprived it of its prey. The sound sent chills up Granddaddy's spine. There was still a reckoning ahead. McGill had promised something in exchange for ten years of good fortune. And payment was due.

They had almost reached the mountain pass where Granddaddy left his mount when the water horse burst through the bushes. It reared over them, hooves striking out in rage. Granddaddy was knocked to the ground and his arm was broke. McGill backed away from the monster, screaming desperate promises of compensation. But the water horse swooped down upon him, its razor-sharp teeth closing around his neck and galloped back through the hedges to its secret pool.

Gasping with pain, Granddaddy bound his broken arm to his side and tried to return to the secret clearing. But the rhododendron tunnel had vanished and so had the smell of brewing whiskey. Even the tiny deer trail was no more. The magic still was gone.

That was when Granddaddy realized that McGill was dead. He'd traded his life for ten years of good fortune and a reputation as the best moonshiner in the hills.

Resources

"A Ghost Club. Weird and Blood Curdling Meeting Place of a Remarkable Organization." Knoxville, TN: *Knoxville Journal*, February 17, 1893.

"A Haunted Spring." Cincinnati, OH: *Cincinnati Commercial Tribune*, February 16, 1890.

"Another Ghost Story. The Ghost of a Murdered Man. Returns Regularly, Making its Appearance the 14th of December of Each Year and Screams for Help." Dallas, TX: *Dallas Morning News*, February 12, 1888.

Appalachian Magazine. Mountain Superstitions, Ghost Stories & Haint Tales. Charleston, West Virginia: StatelyTies Media, 2018.

Arneach, Lloyd. *Long-Ago Stories of the Eastern Cherokee.* Charleston, SC: The History Press, 2008.

Asfar, Daniel. *Ghost Stories of America.* Edmonton, Canada: Ghost House Books, 2001.

Baldwin, Juanitta. *Smoky Mountain Ghostlore.* Kodak, TN: Suntop Press, 2005.

———. *Smoky Mountain Stories.* Kodak, TN: Suntop Press, 2011.

———. *Smoky Mountain Tales, Vol. 1.* Kodak, TN: Suntop Press, 2007.

———. *Smoky Mountain Tales, Vol. 2.* Kodak, TN: Suntop Press, 2008.

Barefoot, Daniel W. *Haints of the Hills.* Winston-Salem, NC: John F. Blair, Publisher, 2002.

Battle, Kemp P. *Great American Folklore.* New York: Doubleday, 1986.

Bayley, Emily Elizabeth. *Folk-Lore of the North Carolina Mountains.* Haithitrust.org. Accessed June 23, 2020. catalog.hathitrust.org/Record/100179101/Home.

Betts, Leonidas, and Richard Walser. *Gateway to North Carolina Folklore*. Raleigh, NC: School of Education Office of Publications, North Carolina State University at Raleigh, 1974.

Bolton, W. Lewis. *Smoky Mountain Jack Tales of Winter and Old Christmas*. Bloomington, IN: Xlibris, 2015.

Botkin, B. A., ed. *A Treasury of American Folklore*. New York: Crown, 1944.

"Bound to Win a Husband." New Bloomfield, PA: *The New Bloomfield Times*, May 7, 1878.

Brown, Alan. *Haunted Tennessee*. Mechanicsburg, PA: Stackpole Books, 2009.

Brown, D. *Legends*. Eugene, OR: Randall V. Mills Archive of Northwest Folklore at the University of Oregon, 1971.

Brunvand, Jan Harold. *The Choking Doberman and Other Urban Legends*. New York: W. W. Norton, 1984.

———. *The Vanishing Hitchhiker*. New York: W. W. Norton, 1981.

Chase, Richard. *Grandfather Tales*. New York: Houghton Mifflin Company, 1948.

———. *The Jack Tales*. New York: Houghton Mifflin Company, 1943.

Coffin, Tristram P., and Hennig Cohen, eds. *Folklore in America*. New York: Doubleday & AMP, 1966.

———. *Folklore from the Working Folk of America*. New York: Doubleday, 1973.

Cohen, Daniel, and Susan Cohen. *Hauntings and Horrors*. New York: Dutton Children's Books, 2002.

Coleman, Christopher K. *Ghosts and Haunts of Tennessee*. Winston-Salem, NC: John F. Blair, Publisher, 2011.

Cooper, Horton. *North Carolina Mountain Folklore and Miscellany*. Murfreesboro, NC: Johnson Publishing, 1972.

"Cricket on the Hearth." St. Joseph, MO: *St. Joseph Herald*, September 20, 1891.

Cross, Tom Peele. "Witchcraft in North Carolina." *Studies in Philology*, 16(3), 217–287. Accessed June 23, 2020. www.jstor.org/stable/4171754.

Curran, Bob. *American Vampires: Their True bloody History from New York to California.* Pompton Plains, NJ: The Career Press, Inc., 2013.

Davis, Donald. *Southern Jack Tales.* Atlanta, GA: August House, Inc., 1992.

Dorson, R. M. *America in Legend.* New York: Pantheon Books, 1973.

Downer, Deborah L. *Classic American Ghost Stories.* Little Rock, AR: August House Publishers, 1990.

Duncan, Barbara R., ed. *Living Stories of the Cherokee.* Chapel Hill, NC: The University of North Carolina Press, 1998.

———. *The Origin of the Milky Way & Other Living Stories of the Cherokee.* Chapel Hill, NC: The University of North Carolina Press, 2008.

Editors of *Life. The Life Treasury of American Folklore.* New York: Time, 1961.

Erdoes, Richard, and Alfonso Ortiz. *American Indian Myths and Legends.* New York: Pantheon Books, 1984.

Farwell, Harold F. Jr., and J. Karl Nicholas, eds. *Smoky Mountain Voices: A Lexicon of Southern Appalachian Speech Based on the Research Of Horace Kephart.* Lexington, KY: The University Press of Kentucky, 1993.

Flanagan, J. T., and A. P. Hudson. *The American Folk Reader.* New York: A. S. Barnes, 1958.

Foxfire Students. *Boogers, Witches, and Haints: Appalachian Ghost Stories. The Foxfire Americana Library.* New York: Anchor Books, 2011.

Foxfire Students. *Mountain Folk Remedies: The Foxfire Americana Library.* New York: Anchor Books, 2011.

Gainer, Patrick W. *Witches, Ghosts and Signs: Folklore of the Southern Appalachians.* Morgantown, WV: West Virginia University Press, 2008.

"Ghost and Goblin. Curious Stories of the World Invisible." Cleveland, OH: *Cleveland Plain Dealer*, January 1, 1888.

Hall, Joseph S. *Smoky Mountain Folks and Their Lore.* Asheville, NC: Gilbert Printing Co., 1960. Published in Cooperation with Great Smoky Mountains Natural History Association.

———. *Yarns and Tales from the Great Smokies*. Asheville, NC: The Cataloochee Press, 1978.

Hardin, John. *The Devil's Tramping Ground and Other North Carolina Mystery Stories*. Chapel Hill: University of North Carolina Press, 1949.

———. *Tar Heel Ghosts*. Chapel Hill: University of North Carolina Press, 1954.

Hauck, Dennis William. *Haunted Places: The National Directory*. New York: Penguin Books, 1996.

Jones, Loyal, and Billy Edd Wheeler. *Curing the Cross-Eyed Mule*. Atlanta, GA: August House Publishers, 1989.

King, Duance H., ed. *The Memoirs of Lt. Henry Timberlake*. Cherokee, NC: Museum of the Cherokee Indian Press, 2007.

Kotarski, Georgiana. *Ghosts of the Southern Tennessee Valley*. Winston-Salem, NC: John F. Blair, 2006.

"Laughing Ghosts." Sacramento, CA: *Themis Vol. III Issue: 13*, May 16, 1891.

Leach, M. *The Rainbow Book of American Folk Tales and Legends*. New York: World Publishing, 1958.

Leeming, David, and Jake Pagey. *Myths, Legends, and Folktales of America*. New York: Oxford University Press, 1999.

"Local Ghost Story. A Sure Enough Mysterious Apparition at Middlebrook." Knoxville, TN: *Knoxville Journal*, August 24, 1894.

MacQueen, Douglas. *Nuckelavee—The Malevolent Creature that Terrorized Scotland's Northern Isles*. Transceltic.com. Accessed June 23, 2020. www.transceltic.com/scottish/nuckelavee-malevolent-creature-terrorised-scotlands-northern-isles.

Manly, Roger. *Weird Carolinas*. New York: Sterling Publishing, 2007.

Mathes, Hodge. *Tall Tales from Old Smoky*. Johnson City, TN: The Overmountain Press, 1991.

Norman, Michael, and Beth Scott. *Historic Haunted America*. New York: Tor Books, 1995.

Norton, Terry L. *Cherokee Myths and Legends: Thirty Tales Retold*. Jefferson, NC: McFarland & Company, Inc., Publishers, 2014.

Ogle, William. *Ghosts of Gatlinburg.* Gatlinburg, TN: Self published, 2015.

Olson, Ted and Anthony P. Cavender, eds. *A Tennessee Folklore Sampler.* Knoxville, TN: University of Tennessee Press, 2009.

Peck, Catherine, ed. *A Treasury of North American Folk Tales.* New York: W. W. Norton, 1998.

Polley, J., ed. *American Folklore and Legend.* New York: Reader's Digest Association, 1978.

Poore, Tammy J. *Ghost Tales & Superstitions of Southern Appalachian Mountains.* Knoxville, TN: Nine Lives Publishing, 2009.

Porter, J. Hampden. *Notes on the Folk-Lore of the Mountain Whites of the Alleghanies.* The *Journal of American Folklore,* 7(25), 105–117. Accessed June 6, 2020. www.jstor.org/stable/533421.

Price, Charles Edwin. *Haints, Witches, and Boogers: Tales from Upper East Tennessee.* Winston-Salem, NC: John F. Blair, Publisher, 1992.

———. *Haunted Tennessee.* Johnson City, TN: The Overmountain Press, 1995.

Renegar, Michael. *Roadside Revenants and Other North Carolina Ghosts and Legends.* Fairview, NC: Bright Mountain Books, 2005.

River, Michael. *Appalachia Mountain Folklore.* Atglen, PA: Schiffer Publishing, Ltd., 2012.

Roberts, Nancy. *Ghosts of the Carolinas.* Columbia, SC: University of South Carolina Press, 1962.

———. *Ghosts of the Southern Mountains and Appalachia.* Columbia, SC: University of South Carolina Press, 1988.

———. *North Carolina Ghosts and Legends.* Columbia, SC: University of South Carolina Press, 1959.

Rule, Leslie. *Coast to Coast Ghosts.* Kansas City, KS: Andrews McMeel Publishing, 2001.

Russell, Randy, and Janet Barnett. *The Granny Curse and Other Ghosts and Legends from East Tennessee.* Durham, NC: Blair, 2011.

———. *Mountain Ghost Stories and Curious Tales of Western North Carolina.* Winston-Salem, NC: John F. Blair, Publisher, 1988.

Schwartz, Alvin. *Scary Stories to Tell in the Dark.* New York: Harper Collins, 1981.

Simmons, Shane S. *Legends & Lore of East Tennessee.* Charleston, SC: History Press, 2016.

"Skinned Tom." Scaryforkids.com. Accessed June 23, 2020. www .scaryforkids.com/skinned-tom.

Skinner, Charles M. *American Myths and Legends.* Vol. 1. Philadelphia: J. B. Lippincott, 1903.

———. *Myths and Legends of Our Own Land.* Vols. 1–2. Philadelphia: J. B. Lippincott, 1896.

Spence, Lewis. *North American Indians: Myths and Legends Series.* London: Bracken Books, 1985.

Still, Laura. *A Haunted History of Knoxville.* Asheville, NC: Stony River Media, 2014.

Students of Haskell Institute. *Myths, Legends, Superstitions of North American Indian Tribes.* Cherokee, NC: Cherokee Publications, 1995.

Thay, Edrick. *Ghost Stories of North Carolina.* Auburn, WA: Lone Pine Publishing International, 2005.

———. *Ghost Stories of the Old South.* Auburn, WA: Lone Pine Publishing International, 2003.

The Nuckelavee—Devil o' the Sea. Orkneyjar.com. Accessed June 1, 2020. www.orkneyjar.com/folklore/nuckle.htm.

"Tim Sullivan's Ghost." Wichita, KS: *The Wichita Daily Eagle*, April 18, 1891.

Traylor, Ken and Delas M. House Jr. *Asheville Ghosts and Legends.* Charleston, SC: Haunted America, 2006.

Walser, Richard. *North Carolina Legends.* Raleigh: Office of Archives and History, North Carolina Department of Cultural History, 1980.

White, Newman Ivey, ed. *The Frank C. Brown Collection of North Carolina Folklore.* Durham, NC: Duke University Press, 1958.

Wigginton, Eliot, ed. and his students. *A Foxfire Christmas.* Chapel Hill, NC: University of North Carolina Press, 1996.

Wigginton, Eliot, ed. and his students. *Foxfire 2*. New York: Anchor Books, 1973.

Wigginton, Eliot, ed. and Margie Bennett. *Foxfire 9*. New York: Anchor Books, 1986.

Wilson, Patty A. *Haunted North Carolina*. Mechanicsburg, PA: Stackpole Books, 2009.

Zeitlin, Steven J., Amy J. Kotkin, and Holly Cutting Baker. *A Celebration of American Family Folklore*. New York: Pantheon Books, 1982.

Zeple, Terrance. *Best Ghost Tales of North Carolina*. Sarasota, FL: Pineapple Press, 2006.

About the Author

S. E. Schlosser has been telling stories since she was a child, when games of "let's pretend" quickly built themselves into full-length tales acted out with friends. A graduate of Houghton College, the Institute of Children's Literature,  and Rutgers University, she created and maintains the award-winning website Americanfolklore.net, where she shares a wealth of stories from all fifty states, some dating back to the origins of America. She spends much of her time answering questions from visitors to the site. Many of her favorite e-mails come from other folklorists who delight in practicing the old tradition of "who can tell the tallest tale."

About the Illustrator

Artist Paul Hoffman trained in painting and printmaking, with his first extensive illustration work on assignment in Egypt, drawing ancient wall reliefs for the University of Chicago. His work graces books of many genres—children's titles, textbooks, short story collections, natural history volumes, and numerous cookbooks. For *Spooky Great Smokies*, he employed a scratchboard technique and an active imagination.